The German Army Medical Corps in World War II
1939-1945

Schiffer Military History
Atglen, PA

Translated from the German by Ed Force

Copyright © 1999 by Schiffer Publishing, Ltd.
Library of Congress Catalog Number: 98-86461

All rights reserved. No part gfi this work may be reproduced or used in any forms or by any means—graphic, electronic or mechanical, including photocopying or information storage and retrieval systems—without written permission from the copyright holder.

Printed in China.
ISBN: 0-7643-0692-8

This book was originally published under the title, *Der Sanitätsdienst des Heeres 1939-1945* by Podzun-Pallas.

We are interested in hearing from authors with book ideas on related topics.

Published by Schiffer Publishing Ltd.
4880 Lower Valley Road
Atglen, PA 19310
Phone: (610) 593-1777
FAX: (610) 593-2002
E-mail: Schifferbk@aol.com
Please visit our web site catalog at www.schifferbooks.com
or write for a free catalog.
This book may be purchased from the publisher.
Please include $3.95 postage.
Try your bookstore first.

Alex Buchner

The German Army Medical Corps in World War II

A Photo Chronicle

CONTENTS

Foreword 5
Introduction 5
General Information—Training 7
Peacetime and Wartime Service 10
Structure and Tasks of the Medical Corps 14
Medical Equipment and Devices 20
Transport Means and Equipment 24
The Army Mountain Medical School 28
Icy Russia and Hot Africa 32
Medical Corps in Action 34
Doctors and Patients Report 59
Hopelessly Surrounded in Action 71
Rescue by Sea 77
To the War's End 85
Statistics, Dates, Facts 86
Bibliography 88
Illustrations 89

FOREWORD

It is not the sense or purpose of the book before you to take a lesson or draw a moral on the work of the medical corps of the German Army in World War II, to discuss specialist information or go into the realm of wartime medicine. Rather it is meant to be an understandable portrayal of the lives of those doctors and medics of the field army who—like any other soldiers—served at the front in order to provide help and rescue when needed. For reasons of the book's extent, the medical services of the replacement army, particularly that of the many deserving Red Cross nurses, had to be omitted, although they also served in military hospitals. The medical corps of the Navy and Luftwaffe also had to be omitted, although the paratroops have been mentioned, since they fought on the ground like all other Army units. The author, wounded three times himself, is well aware that this book thus has numerous gaps. Corrections and completions will be accepted with gratitude.

Thanks for their kind assistance in research are hereby expressed to the Schild-Verlag of Munich, to Koehlers Verlagsgesellschaft of Herford, and to the Verlag der "Deutschen Militärschrift" in Brühl.

Alex Buchner

INTRODUCTION

In times of peace, the medical corpsmen of all ranks—the "Sanis"—have often been satirized as "pill-rollers" or the like, and every German soldier knew the song of Medical Corporal Neumann and his Miracle Salve. There were also many jokes about the staff doctors, and the saying: "Iodine on the outside, aspirin on the inside, that's all you need."

But then, when things got serious and one had to go to war, and the fights and battles and slaughters got worse and worse, especially in the eastern campaign, countless soldiers called for the "Sani"! Thus "Sani" soon became an honorable name for all medical ranks, medics, stretcher bearers and doctors alike, to whom many entrusted their lives in the rescue of the sick and wounded.

The selfless achievements under great pressure that were required of and performed by the members of the medical corps are not inferior to those of the fighting forces. Only the best-trained and most experienced doctors and medical personnel could fulfill their hard tasks. The comradely closeness and the trust of the combat troops were always with them.

The men of the medical corps, always eager to serve, fulfilled their tasks with determination and self-sacrifice. The medics and stretcher bearers often went into enemy fire to rescue the wounded and gave first aid during combat. Day and night the ambulance drivers were underway, usually on the worst roads, to bring back the sick and wounded as quickly as possible. In like manner, the doctors and their helpers did their duty under the most turbulent conditions at troop bandaging stations and in hospitals, without rest and to the point of exhaustion, until the last patients were treated.

The men with the emblem of Aesculapius and the red-cross armband did everything they could to help, and they helped wherever and whenever they could.

Hundreds of thousands of German soldiers owe their lives and health to the doctors and medics.

Medical Officers of the Army
Insignia of Rank

1. Unterarzt; the corresponding military rank was Oberfähnrich. Shoulder patches of blue-dark green fabric with aluminum frame and cornflower-blue border, stars and staff of metallic white.
2-7. Shoulder patches of flat aluminum thread with cornflower-blue border, gold stars and staff.
2. Assistenzarzt, equal to Leutnant
3. Oberarzt   Oberleutnant
4. Stabsarzt   Hauptmann
5. Oberstabarzt   Major
6. Oberfeldarzt   Oberstleutnant
7. Oberstarzt   Oberst
8-10. Shoulder patches with a weave of two gold cords and one silver cord, underlaid by red (like generals of the army), metallic white star and staff.
8. Generalarzt   Generalmajor
9. Generalstabsarzt   Generalleutnant
10. Generaloberstabsarzt   General

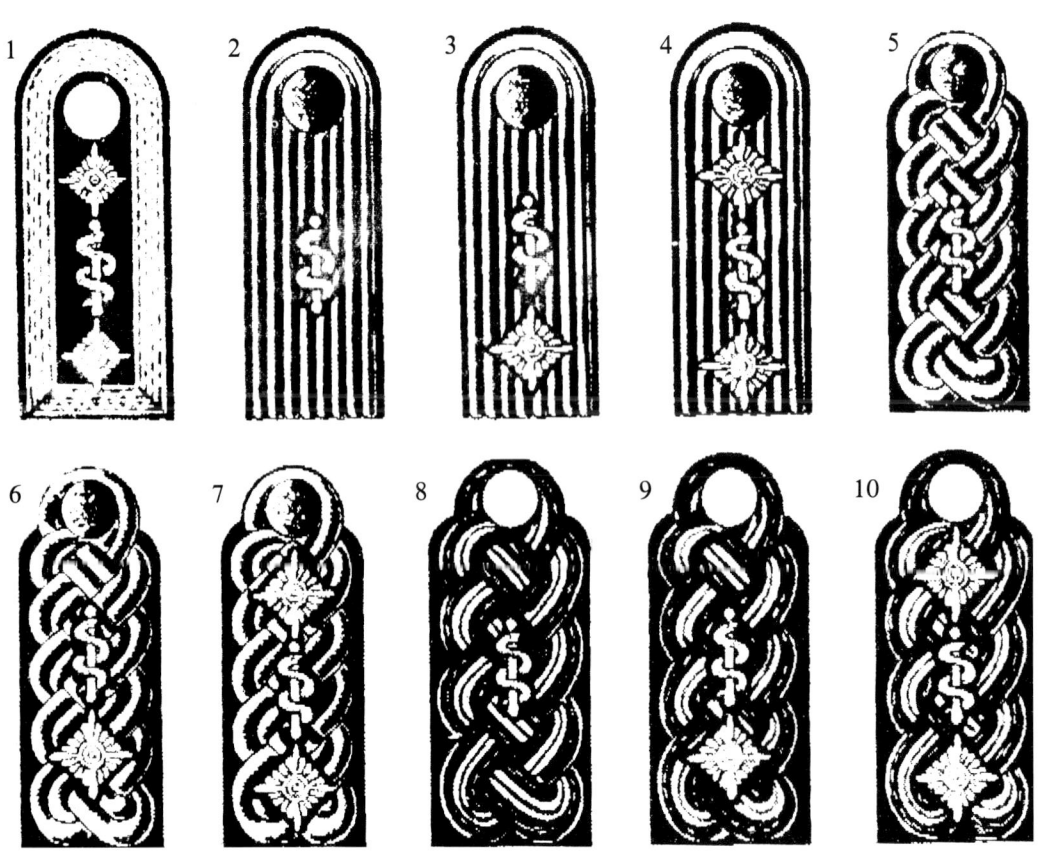

General Information—Training

The medical corps of the army was divided into the medical services for the field and replacement armies, in troop units and hospitals, from large units like army groups to small ones like battalions, belonging to divisions of various types, such as infantry, mountain divisions, etc.

They were neither a type of troop nor a service arm, but had a cornflower-blue emblem color and had typical army organization, structure and designations.

The names of ranks for medical officers, though, were different (see previous page), and they wore additional shoulder patches with the staff of Aesculapius. The emblems of rank for medical officers and corpsmen were like those of the other troops, but prefixed with the term "Sanitäts," "Sanitätssoldat," "Sanitätsfeldwebel," etc. They were all simply called "Sanis" by the troops, and the doctors were called "Doktor."

All of the medical corpsmen wore the same field-gray uniform and equipment as all the other German soldiers, but added a red cross armband on the left sleeve of their uniforms.

All members of the medical corps were under the protection of the Geneva Convention of 1929 (Convention to improve the lot of wounded and sick of the army in the field). It had been ratified, with its definitions of protection, by Germany in 1934.

According to a directive from the Army High Command (OKH) of May 23, 1939, according to which all Wehrmacht personnel were combatants, the members of the medical corps were also armed, with pistols as well as 98k rifles. According to the Geneva Convention, they had the right, in case of and for the duration of urgent danger, to defend themselves and persons in their care (wounded and sick) with those weapons. They were not allowed to be either attacked or fired on, nor to be involved in ground, air, or sea combat. Therefore they were to wear their red-cross armbands clearly visible on their uniforms. The red cross also was to be attached, visible from a distance, on buildings, tents, vehicles, etc., used for medical purposes, or these were to be marked with flags. They could be used only for the treatment, housing and transport of the wounded and sick.

The Geneva Convention went on to state principles of the application and following of the rules, as well as misuse of the red cross symbol to the advantage of the combat troops. On the other hand, the Convention provided neither international control nor means of punishment in cases of abuse.

The importance and significance of the medical service of the Army emphasizes its growth in the war years. Despite the great need for doctors in civilian life, and the needs of the Luftwaffe and Navy, the numbers were:

In the first war year of 1939-40, there were 7,798 doctors and 92,348 medical corpsmen with the troops in the field army, 1,314 medical officers and 9,731 medical soldiers in hospitals.

In the fourth war year of 1942-43, there were 17,034 medical officers and 164,898 men with the troops, 4,689 doctors and 28,737 medical corpsmen in hospitals. In addition, the replacement army had 9,507 doctors and 53,438 medical personnel.

Here is an indication of their effect:

Apart from the slight cases who recuperated with the troops, of the wounded men sent to field hospitals in 1942-43, some 47.7% returned to the front capable of service. In the reserve hospitals, some 3.5% returned directly to their front units, 72% were transferred to the replacement troops and, after some time, returned to the field with so-called "marching battalions," while about 24.5% remained capable only of garrison service or were mustered completely out of service with permanent injuries.

Included in these figures are the wounded, injured, and sick. There was a clear distinction between the first two:
- Wounds resulted from enemy action;
- Injuries resulted from accidents.

In their training, the path to becoming a medical officer (military doctor) of the Army will be described briefly. It began in peacetime after a number of semesters of medical training (study time), with a voluntary enlistment and stationing as a medical officer's orderly. Then the path led to the troops for infantry training, which lasted about eight months. After this time, the progressing medical officers attended the Military Medical Academy in Berlin as their training base. At first they held the rank of Fahnenjunker, then of Fähnrich in the medical corps, and attended lectures in their subject at the nearby Charité. After their state examination came their Unterarzt training at the Academy. These lower-rank (Oberfähnrich) doctors, like their civilian colleagues, then spent a year in practice at large clinics, leading to their certification. At the level of Unterarzt they were not yet qualified as medical officers. Their daytime activities in the clinics were accompanied by lectures by staff doctors and the like at the Academy. In this year they also wrote their doctoral dissertation, and at the end of the year they took an examination. With the receipt of their certification and title of doctor, they were transferred to garrisons with the rank of Assistenzarzt (Leutnant).

The path followed by Army druggists was similar.

During the war, young, newly trained doctors followed this path and then spent their practical year in front service with the combat troops.

In general, high ability and knowledge of all branches of their work were demanded and achieved. Surgical treatment and medical methods that one would not have had to choose in peacetime often had to be applied in the war, and at times they brought unexpected success.

The training of the medical officers and corpsmen at the Army medical schools was very intensive, and the requirements were very high.

The certificate of completed training was the Dv. 59. The introductory words from it, as it stood on August 12, 1939, are as follows:

"The service of the medical officers and corpsmen in peacetime include first aid, the care of the sick and injured, the support of medical officers, maintenance of medical equipment and supplies."

This Dv. 59 consisted of 431 pages and 194 illustrations and included extensive material. It extended from the structure of the human body through illnesses and injuries in accidents (not wounds from enemy action) of all kinds and treatments, to resuscitation and bandaging instructions, to the care of the sick. Service in the hospital, the x-ray department and the pharmacy were included. The trainees also had to know all the customary instruments and their uses, so that in time of need they could assist in operations. There was as yet nothing stated about wounds in wartime.

After finishing the first training course and passing the examination, the trainee was allowed to wear a round emblem with the staff of Aesculapius on his lower right arm.

Like the medical officers, all ranks of the medical corps were required to keep absolute discretion. If complete readiness to serve was required of them in peacetime, full personal devotion was required in wartime.

The training of the entire medical corps and the preparation of the medical service in time of war were likewise a part of the medical corps in peacetime. But an extensive training of medical officers and personnel in modern war medicine, and particularly in war surgery, could scarcely be provided, since experience resulted only from World War I and, in a few cases, from the 1936-39 Spanish Civil War.

During the war, training times for all medical personnel were shortened. It cannot be denied, though, that during barracks training many useless drills, such as the assembly of field stretchers, were part of the exercises.

And it should also be noted that there was even a dog school in Berlin for medical-corps and messenger dogs.

Doctors and all other medical personnel became the best friends of the combat troops. They exuded self-assurance, confidence and consolation as if there were no difficulties in saving all the young men who hovered between life and death. Often enough, they also had to be people without nerves when twenty to thirty operations a day had to be performed at field bandaging stations and field hospitals, and numerous measures had to be taken to preserve life.

Staff Suregon Dr. Wilcke, the first Army doctor to win the Knight's Cross.

Peacetime and Wartime Service

In times of peace they were already found in the musterings and organizational examinations in the sickbays of the barracks. When a "drafted" soldier reported sick to the UvD (Unteroffizier vom Dienst) after reveille and was brought to the sickbay with the company's sick report book, to find sick men from other companies already waiting, one was immediately received by the helping and healing "demigods of medicine."

As a rule, every battalion or unit had a sickbay, which was directed by a medical officer (Assistenzarzt, Stabsarzt, etc.), and to which the medical enlisted men were assigned, after six months of military basic training with the troops and after finishing training and passing a test at a medical school. In the sickbay, they took care of the patients. In addition, they supplied the medical service's first aid to the companies and batteries in major drills, maneuvers, etc., while the troop doctor was present for the battalion's or unit's drills. In terms of supplies (clothing, provisions, pay, etc.), they always belonged to a certain troop unit.

Taking place in the sickbays were medical examination, medical treatment and care of the sick or injured soldiers, and often of their family members. The equipping of the consulting and treating room with medical equipment corresponded to that of a comparable civilian doctor. Along with walk-in care, stationary reception of the patient was often possible as well if there was no hospital in the city, or if transfer to a hospital was not necessary.

Among the tasks of the military doctor, there were also the advising of the troop leaders, supervision of hygienic measures in the housing area (kitchen, canteen, toilets), and sick-calls. In places with several medical officers, the one with the longest service was the local doctor. He was the medical advisor of the local chief and regulated the medical services at the locality.

All medical officers and enlisted men formed the medical staff of the locality and were members of a medical unit.

The commander of each medical unit was the division doctor. For all those soldiers in the medical service he was the man in command. For the whole division, he was responsible to the division commander for all medical matters in the health sector of the troops.

In peacetime there had been no mobile medical units. Only for large-scale maneuvers were drill medical companies established. For the military actions in Austria in March 1938, in the Sudetenland in October 1938, and in Czechoslovakia in March 1939 as well, there was organizational training, but medical services were not necessary, as the few sick and injured men could be treated sufficiently in the local hospitals.

With the mobilization at the end of August 1939, numerous medical units including hospitals had to be set up. Thus small cadres of local medical personnel joined those troop units that they had already been assigned to economically in peacetime. To these active medical officers and personnel, who naturally were not enough, large numbers of enlisted men were added to fill them out, but there was a shortage of trained personnel. As quickly as possible, these medical units had to train men, especially those from first-aid stations, lower-ranking clergy, monks, etc., to prepare them for their tasks. Their training by doctors and medical corpsmen was continued between their first active services. It was much better for doctors from civilian life, many of whom had been called into service as reserves, as they were trained already. Among them were numerous practicing doctors, medical men of all kinds from private practice, clinics and even universities.

At first there were enough surgeons, internists, anesthetists, orthopedics, eye, ear, nose and throat doctors, hygienists, pharmacists, chemists, psychologists and the like. Their knowledge was based on central European conditions. It was different when, in 1941, German troops had to wage war in North Africa. Here doctors had to be trained for tropical conditions, since none were available at first. There were, at first, also many shortages of equipment, supplies and vehicles. Thus many units went to war with makeshift vehicles and could only be fully supplied with captured vehicles.

Through the division doctors, the mobilizing units for the troop medical services were set up, particularly the medical units of the divisions, which will be discussed at length below.

At the head of the Army Medical Service was the Heeres-Sanitätainspekteur with the rank of a Generaloberstabsarzt. Since the war began, he and his staff were located in the Army Office. As the representative of by far the largest branch of the Wehrmacht, he was simultaneously responsible for the medical services of the entire Wehrmacht. He was also the senior advisor of the Military High Command (OKW) for matters invloving medical services.

Along with his coordinating responsibilities for the medical services of the Wehrmacht until 1944, the Heeres-Sanitätsinspekteur was the commander of all the Army's medical personnel and responsible for the conduct of medical services in the Army. Also subordinate to him were the main medical facility in Berlin, the central supply office for medical supplies, and the Military Medical Academy.

The Army Medical Inspection consisted of the personnel department, organizational department with procurement, transport and supply services, science and health department (epidemic protection, gas protection, etc.), and other agencies.

The Heeres-Arzt (Generalstabsarzt) was the leading medical officer of the field army with the Quartermaster General of the Army High Command (OKH). His job was directing the medical services of the field army according to the directives of the Sanitätsinspekteur. In all theaters of war he was responsible for the availability of the required medical services, and he regulated the movements of the wounded and sick to the backline facilities. To do this, he commanded his own Army medical forces, such as medical units, field and reserve hospitals, patient transport units, etc., that could be deployed where needed. In addition, he always had to prepare the reports of casualties.

Directly subordinate to the Heeres-Arzt were five high-ranking medical officers in the occupied countries (France, Belgium, the Balkans, the East, and the Ukraine).

The advising specialist doctors of the Wehrmacht were also at his side. As of 1941, the two offices of Sanitätsinspekteur and Heeres-Arzt were united under the Heeresarzt.

For the field army in the war zones, from the command level downward there followed the Referate IV b in the quartermaster units of the army groups, armies, corps and divisions. They took care of and were responsible for all medical needs among the appropriate high active medical officers and their staffs. To do so, they received the tactical commands, directives and instructions from their command staffs, the staffs of the next higher medical superiors. To carry out their tasks, medical units of varying numbers and strengths were detailed to them.

Army Group Doctors (Generalärzte): They directed front hospital units consisting of two front hospitals (motorized), two slight-case front hospitals and two patient transport units each. In the front hospitals (also in the armies), all medical facilities were under the command of the best specialist doctors, and a supply of some 500 beds, which could be expanded to 1,000, was available. Front hospital bases in the east had a capacity of 4,000 to 6,000 beds. The transport units handled the practical assignment and transportation of the patients. There were also facilities for medical research.

Army Doctors (Generalärzte or Oberstärzte) had command of a large and sometimes varying number of medical services. As a rule, they commanded Army medical units of six army front hospitals (also usable as epidemic hospitals), two medical companies, each with some 200 men, six ambulance platoons, and one amy medical park with three platoons. These medical units could be deployed, if needed, in the rear portion of the front area and assigned to the corps and vision doctors for support.

Corps Doctors (Oberstärzte): Only as of 1943 were they assigned a small number of their own medical units.

Division Doctors (Oberfeldärzte) or Oberstärzte): Closed medical units were in the divisions, as medical units directly with the troops.

Defense Zone Doctors in the replacement army were responsible particularly for the health care and maintenance of the replacement units. In their zones there were also homeland and reserve hospitals, which constantly increased in numbers with the duration of the war and the recession of the fronts in the war.

To state statistics here, in Defense Zone VII (Old Bavaria) there were, in March 1945, 76 reserve hospitals with 289 partial hospitals, which accepted wounded brought to them by the field army. In Garmisch alone, there were about 10,000 wounded in May 1945. The hospitals located in towns were, despite orders to the contrary, largely turned over to the advancing Americans as hospital cities.

A special and important role was played by the groups of advisory high-ranking doctors, with significant and well-known names, located with the Medical inspection, the army groups and armies of the field army, as well as in the defense zones of the replacement army. Among them were, for example, the great surgeon Geheimrat Professor Dr. Sauerbruch, who, already a Generalarzt and bearer of the Knight's Cross, was decorated with the Kriegsverdienstkreuz. These experts held a military and medical meeting at the Military Medical Academy in Berlin on January 3 and 4, 1940.

Staff Doctor von Günther, chief of a medical company, wrote about them at the end of 1941:

"We received a surprise visit from the "advisory" surgeon of our army, the famous Viennese accident surgeon Professor Dr. Böhler. There were very lively discussions, especially with my surgeons. Differences of opinion between surgical procedures at home in peacetime and surgical procedures in the front-line areas came out very clearly. There was agreement that the purpose of all surgical treatments must be the heightening of the wounded man's chance of survival. Both sides also agreed that a wounded man, after primary wound treatment, should be taken as quickly and as gently as possible to the back-line medical facilities." Different views on treatment in bandaging stations arose, though, in the question of the time and extent of amputations and the like, whether because of shell or shell-fragment wounds or freezing. There was also much discussion of the treatment of bones broken by shots, methods of treating wounds and shock, bandaging techniques and use of narcotics.

"An essential topic of discussion was asepsis, for antibiotics and sulfonamide were not yet available. Nor was it possible to take X-rays at the bandaging stations. In addition, decisions about the most life-threatening conditions, particularly those of abdominal and chest wounds, generally had to be made more quickly at the front lines than in civilian life. One facet that came out of the discussion was that every decision made by a surgeon included a certain quotient of error."

Comrades help out on the front line.

Structure and Tasks of the Medical Corps

This chapter is dedicated primarily to the medical services among the troops.

The task of these medical units was the complete care of all wounded and sick in the entire sphere of action of each division, through the establishment of troop bandaging stations, collecting points, main bandaging stations and field hospitals, as well as transportation to the back-line army zones. Naturally, wounded from other divisions were given the same care when necessary. This troop medical service began with stretcher bearers and medics with more or less good training. Every rifle platoon (or equivalent) had in its platoon troop a medical soldier equipped with two medical kits. They treated minor injuries, such as blistered feet, bodily abrasions, diarrhea, nausea, sunstroke, etc. In combat, they were—backed up by soldiers as temporary stretcher bearers when needed—present in the front lines, sought and located wounded soldiers and brought them, often under enemy fire, to so-called "nests of the wounded" located in places sheltered by the terrain. There they performed first aid, put on bandages, treated wounded limbs and applied pressure bandages for heavy bleeding. In addition, they arranged for further transport and took patients unable to walk, on stretchers or otherwise—unless fellow soldiers did this—to troop bandaging stations. Slightly wounded men had to get there themselves.

In every company the immediate superior of the troop medics was a medical non-commissioned officer or sergeant, along with a medical corpsman. In combat, they were located with the battalion doctor and formed his staff at the troop bandaging station. All battalions or units already had a medical officer (Assistenz- or Oberarzt = Truppenarzt = Bataliionsarzt) with two medical corpsmen. Among his tasks in quiet times were advising the troop leader of all medical needs, temporary measures against diseases and epidemics by issuing certain medicines (for instance, atabrine and quinine, malaria medicines known to many soldiers), checking the food at the field kitchens, supervision of hygienic measures in barrack areas, latrines, garbage dumps, removal of cadavers, etc., as well as occasional health announcements, training on medical service subjects, and ongoing training of the medical personnel.

On the march, the battalion doctor carried necessary medicines and implements for serious cases with him in a large medical kit. Needles for injections were kept sterile in a small container filled with alcohol.

In combat the troop doctor and his staff set up the troop bandaging station (TVP) at a suitable place, just out of enemy infantry fire but still within range of the artillery, easy to reach and as covered as possible, often in the vicinity of the battalion command post. Suitable places included farmyards with barns and a well, plus (especially in winter) well-dug bunkers, safe from enemy fire. Here the medical equipment a), which also included surgical instruments for minor surgery, was available to the troop doctor. Of course there were no facilities for operating at the troop bandaging stations, but sometimes it had to be done all the same. With the support of his staff, the doctor's tasks included, as a rule, the first proper treatment, checking, renewing and improving bandages of wounds, giving medicine to strengthen heartbeat and respiration, as well as refreshing and thirst-quenching drinks, plus pain-killing injections, and staunching heavy bleeding. Naturally, injections to prevent tetanus were also given.

All means and measures should help provide transport to a main bandaging station as soon as possible. Slightly wounded men were sent on their way to a gathering place.

Important factors, therefore, were examination and judgment of ability to be transported, preparation for it as well as provision of vehicles and carriers. The patient's tag played a major role here. Carefully filled out and hung on the wounded soldier in plain sight, it accompanied him from his first treatment to a hospital back home. It gave information in short form on personal data, type of wound, and important treatment or medicines received. This tag made of stiff paper had a red strip, which could be torn off, on each side. If it was complete, it meant "minor injuries, fully able to be transported, including seated." If one stripe was removed, it meant "transport only lying down"—usually a badly wounded man. If both stripes were removed, it meant very seriously wounded and not transportable, or only under particular conditions, such as in a Fieseler Storch airplane.

Among the troop doctors there was also the regimental doctor, usually a Stabsarzt or Oberstabsarzt. He supervised the battalion doctors, the medical facilities in the companies, battalions and regiment, directed the transport of sick and wounded, saw to necessary supplying of medical materials, and was in direct contact with the division doctor. The regimental doctor could, in times of combat, also utilize the regimental musicians as stretcher bearers and medical personnel. Later the longest-serving battalion doctor also took on the function of the regimental doctor.

From here on the medical services of the division began. It noteworthy that these services were not gathered into one single unit, and thus they had no commander or staff. The individual units were commanded by medical officers. The director and commander of all medical services was the division doctor.

As a rule, the medical services of a division had a total strength of sixteen medical officers (doctors) and 500 men, including:

1st Medical Company (horsedrawn), with six medical officers, two officials, 160 NCOs and men (such as medical NCOs and soldiers, stretcher bearers, care personnel, drivers, etc.), plus 17 horsedrawn vehicles, 45 horses, one car, one truck, one solo and one sidecar motorcycle, and one bicycle echelon.

2nd Medical Company (motorized), with six medical officers, three officials, 157 medical NCOs and men, with four cars, 21 trucks, two solo and four sidecar motorcycles.

Every medical company was led by a Stabsarzt or Oberstabsarzt as company chief and consisted of the leader group (chief doctor and doctors), intelligence echelon and three platoons. In the later course of the war there was also a fourth (delousing) platoon. In addition, in Poland and the western campaign in 1939 and 1940, canine echelons with medical dogs from the military medical canine school in Berlin were also used.

The duties of the two medical companies either relieved or overlapped each other, meaning that the following company on the march either took over an already established bandaging station or marched past it and set up a new one.

The first platoon of every medical company, led by an internist, was the stretcher-carrier platoon. It helped the medical corpsmen and temporary stretcher bearers to search the battlefield for wounded. In action, this platoon also set up vehicle stops (occupied by one NCO), in order to take sick and wounded from troop bandaging stations and other medical facilities and transport them to a main bandaging station in horsedrawn or motor vehicles. In mobile warfare, this platoon also looked after collecting spots for sick and wounded, in occupied by a medical NCO, to move patients farther back.

The second platoon was the main bandaging station platoon. It was led by a surgeon. The platoon, with a strength of circa 45 men, set up a main bandaging station (HV-Platz). To do so, it could form one or two operation groups. An OP group was made up of: 1 surgeon, 1 or 2 physicians, one instrument assistant, one anesthetist, 1 sterilizer (medical NCOs) as operation assistants, and one care group.

The platoon had a complete set of operating implements packed in its medical kit, with a complete lighting system and a light field X-ray unit, as well as what was needed for patient care.

A main bandaging station was located 6 to 10 kilometers behind the front (more or less out of range of heavy weapons and light artillery), in order to guarantee as undisturbed treatment as possible. In mobile war it was only set up when the combat situation and the number of wounded made it necessary, and in defensive war, it was usually set up as soon as possible. Suitable places were rigid buildings, including cellars, or the medical company's tents, set up outdoors.

Prescribed for smooth functioning were: a command post with communications station, housing for personnel, approach and exit routes for vehicles coming from the front, plus an unloading place, reception, bandaging and operating departments, waiting room for wounded able to march, rooms for newly operated patients, wounded and sick who were or were not able to be transported, room for the dying, covered parking places for vehicles, routes to the hinterland, dentist's office, space for the field kitchen, and latrines.

The HV-Platz was the most important place for general wound treatment, and the first place at which complete medical help was available. After an important examination, its main task was performing life-saving treatment, in order to prepare the patients for further transport.

The first priority was setting up a reception area directed by a medical NCO to determine the records and conduct the first examination of the patients, as well as the bandaging room, usually under the direction of the internist, for slightly wounded men, that could be used for checking and replacing bandages, and also for necessary eye and ear examinations, and if necessary, as an extra operating room. The groups of surgeons worked in the actual operating room. It was their duty to recognize immediately, out of a large number of wounded, those who urgently needed surgery and to carry out the needed procedures. The average operation time for a seriously wounded man was 30 minutes to one hour. The doctors were capable of carrying out even the more difficult operations, such as for abdominal, head or lung wounds. Badly injured limbs were handled just as carefully as bones broken by shots, with splints and the like. All the seriously wounded and ill were placed appropriately after their treatment, cared for and prepared for further transport.

A formed medical sergeant wrote: "Soon ambulances brought all the badly wounded to the main bandaging station. There they were first placed in medical tents or in available, prepared houses, often side by side, scarcely 20 to 25 years old. By their medical tags the surgeons could get an idea of the types and seriousness of their wounds and thus set up the sequence in which the wounded came to the operating table. Again there were injections (against tetanus, gas edema, gas burn infections, etc.). Here, where the whole pain and misery of war were revealed massively and mercilessly, screaming was rarely heard, only the suppressed groaning of several badly wounded men."

Every wounded man, within the first six hours, was supposed to reach a main bandaging station or be taken there, but this, because of transport difficulties, was often not possible. This passage of time not only led to a worsening of the wounds, but also caused the dangerous "phlegmone" (gas burn), with fatal results.

When necessary, advanced NV stations could also be set up.

Under strong pressure, especially in times of large-scale combat, the main as well as the troop bandaging stations could be only way stations on the road to the hinterlands.

The third platoon of every medical company, likewise led by a surgeon when possible, was the replacement platoon and carried spare equipment and materials. This platoon provided needed replacement personnel for the other two platoons and established gathering stations for the slightly ill or injured. It was also trained for the care of those injured in chemical warfare.

In addition, the medical company had a dental station with a dentist and assistant.

In every medical company there was also a field pharmacy with all the necessary medicines. The pharmacy was led by an army pharmacist (official) and a pharmacist's assistant (medical NCO). The so-called "pharmacy kit b)" was carried on a 3.5-ton truck.

The army pharmacists not only dispensed prepared medicines but were also occupied in the preparation of types of medicine in solid and liquid forms of all kinds, such as salves, powders, tablets, pills, solutions, tinctures, etc. They also carried out tests of foodstuffs and other tests and played a decisive role in avoiding epidemics.

They were also responsible for the supplying of equipment to the medical units. Army pharmacists, like all other members of the medical corps, often did everything possible, under the most difficult conditions, to supply the sick and wounded sufficiently with medicines.

In addition, every medical company included a paymaster, writing room and commissary group with field kitchen and kitchen personnel. At least one cook among them had to be capable of preparing diet food.

Each of the two medical companies had the personnel and equipment to set up two main bandaging stations.

In the medical services of the divisions there was also a motorized field hospital with an Oberstabsarzt as its chief, five medical officers, four officials (one dentist, one pharmacist, two paymasters) and 66 men as medical personnel, and six cars, 12 trucks and two sidecar cycles as vehicles. Among the medical officers there were at least two surgeons and one specialist doctor for internal illnesses. In addition to the medical personnel, there were sometimes also Red Cross nurses. The entire field hospital was divided into a command unit, first and second platoons. Field hospitals were located at least 20 to 25 kilometers behind the front, usually outside the combat zone and beyond the range of normal weapons. They were often set up in existing hospitals, schools or suitable large houses. It was also possible to set them up in large tents, like HV stations. Like those stations, they also had reception and bandaging rooms, several large operating rooms with specialized diagnosis and therapy facilities, X-ray and pharmacy rooms, treatment and care rooms and a dental station. There were also the kitchen and supply areas as well as a morgue. Medical supplies and foodstuffs were brought in from a medical park.

The field hospitals were set up to hold 200 sick and wounded, but they could handle up to 300 seriously wounded, and if necessary even more.

They followed their divisions during advances, thus the wounded were transferred as quickly as possible to a back-line army hospital, or the army hospital replaced the field hospital during the advance.

The field hospitals were the centers of medical treatment, particularly of surgical and internist care of the badly wounded and sick. With stationary reception, they offered a place to stay for a limited time, the best medical treatment, sufficient attention and care in special departments, in beds or at least on straw sacks. In the field hospitals, care was given to all those cases that could not be handled by the medical companies in their main bandaging stations near the front. For all the wounded and sick, the necessary treatment was carried out under almost peacetime conditions, corresponding to a good civilian hospital.

Operations often had to go on without pause for two or three days. A surgery team with two or three doctors could give treatment to 30 badly, 60 moderately or 120 slightly wounded men in 24 hours.

In the dental station, 40 to 50 patients could be treated in a day.

For example, a mobile field hospital, located near Stalingrad in September 1942, treated 600 to 800 wounded a day and moved them across the Volga.

The staffs of the field hospitals were also involved in drinking-water supplying with their own drinking-water preparation facilities, and in prevention of disease and insect pests (delousing stations). For infectious diseases such as dysentery, malaria or typhus, special temporary isolation stations were set up. The field hospitals, though, had too few personnel, and in vigorous mobile warfare in times of advance or withdrawal, they were sometimes superfluous and were replaced by main bandaging stations. What with their frequent relocation, patients who could not be transported nevertheless had to be sent farther back.

From 1942 on, the field hospitals were generally turned over to the armies by the divisions, but could be reassigned if necessary.

The new structure of Infantry Division 43 no longer called for a field hospital, but there were two more medical companies and one ambulance company.

Finally, the medical services of the divisions included two ambulance platoons, led by an Oberleutnant or Leutnant and composed of three groups of 40 men each, with five ambulances (Sankas) plus two cars and eight sidecar motorcycles each. The ambulance platoons were also independent units and were directly subordinate to the division doctor, who also regulated their duties. The platoons had the task of bringing wounded and sick from the troop and main bandaging stations, gathering points, etc., to the field hospital or other back-line hospitals, to hospital platoons, medical aircraft or hospital ships. As needed, they were often sent out from vehicle stopping places, or detailed temporarily to the battalion or regimental doctors to transport wounded and sick.

In the often extensive division zones, the ambulance crews were often on their own, on the road night and day, in any weather, on the worst roads, and also under enemy fire. Red cross flags were mounted to show that they had wounded on board.

The division doctor was the leader of Unit IV b in the division staff (quartermaster unit). With him were two medical officers and three medical NCOs.

He was the immediate superior of the medical services and of all the medical personnel in the division. He directed marching movements and focal-point action of the medical companies, the field hospital and the ambulance platoons for the treatment and transport of wounded and sick soldiers in the division zone, and their further transport to the rear. His duty area also included health regulations, hygienic measures for the troops and the civilian population, supervision and control of illness situations and measures to prevent epidemics. He also received the reports about the establishment of HV stations and field hospitals and their readiness.

He had the Kit B supplies of medical equipment, which he could issue on request.

To refer briefly to the organization of the mountain troops and paratroops, a medical unit with a strength of about 550 men consisted, similarly to that of an infantry division, of two medical companies (partly motorized) of three platoons each, with one chief doctor, 4 to 6 doctors, one pharmacist, medical soldiers, stretcher bearers and drivers, with a total strength of 184 men each. Each company had two transport platoons, could set up a main bandaging station and form one or two operating groups. It also had its own high mountain platoons with beast-of-burden echelons.

A field hospital (partly motorized) with a strength of 91 men was usually housed in permanent buildings and could hold about 200 patients.

Two ambulance columns (motorized) with ambulances had three platoons, each with 22 men.

Among the medical units there were also the medical groups of the battalions with one Assistenzarzt, one medical Feldwebel and 8 to 10 medical soldiers or stretcher bearers. They set up the troop bandaging stations as far forward as possible.

In the mountains, where there were great distances between troop and main bandaging stations, medical support points were set up. They had a medical NCO with several helpers to care for wounded and sick who passed through, change bandages if necessary, find housing, etc.

The medical units of the paratroops went through various changes during the war. In the Cretan campaign of 1941 they consisted of:

- Paratroop Medical Company 7 in the 7th Paratroop Division,
- One medical unit of three companies, and
- One airborne hospital of the XI. Flying Corps.

All units could land by parachute or be landed by aircraft. Care of the wounded, with overlapping action of all medical services, had to begin as far forward as possible, with all medical units working only rearward. In a determined order, wounded and sick had to find complete treatment, better care and finally complete recovery. Their way led from the "nest of the wounded," on foot or carried, to the troop bandaging stations. From there it led by vehicle (usually ambulance) to the HV station or, for the slightly wounded, on foot to the gathering place for them. From there they went on foot or with empty columns to the gathering place for the sick. Here they joined slightly wounded men from the HV stations and field hospitals. While the transport of sick or slightly wounded by auxiliary hospital platoons went from gathering places, either directly or via gathering places at military hospitals, to the reserve hospitals back home, the badly wounded were taken by ambulance to military hospitals and then by rail, plane or ship to reserve or homeland hospitals. The number of beds in these hospitals at the beginning of 1943 was 800,000. The purpose of this chain, after first aid or care by comrades, was supposed to be quick treatment at the bandaging stations and then quick transport for intensive and long-term treatment of the wounded and sick in the hospitals.

Medical Equipment and Devices

The equipment—especially of the troop medical services—had to be created and organized at its best in all units of the field army. Thus it was important for transport (of equipment and supplies), including over long distances, to use uniform wooden packing cases, clearly marked, for uniformly space-saving packaging, separating bandages, medicines and equipment, all safely packed yet easy to pack and unpack quickly. A certain uniformity of the equipment and its use was also called for. The means of transport for large equipment included horsedrawn and motor vehicles. The most important medical supplies, instruments and equipment will be described briefly below.

Medical supplies ultimately belonged to every soldier, for each possessed a large and a small first aid kit, as well as, originally, a package of losantin to use for possible chemical wounds, but that soon was thrown into a ditch somewhere, as it was never used. The situation was different from the start with packages of bandages. They were urgently needed, but a serious shortage showed up with their use as well. While there were often ineffective attempts at bandaging, the soldiers had practically no medical training. Thus bandages were often put on wrong, for many men had no idea of how to bandage properly or to transport wounded comrades.

Field medical equipment began with the frequently used stretcher-bearers' kits used by the foot soldiers. They consisted of two leather cases, the left one with gauze bandages and strips (pressed to save space), packages of bandages and bandaging cloth, adhesive tape, safety pins, plus medical forceps, scissors and fingernail cleaners in a special container. In the right pouch were bandages and bandaging cloth, watertight bandages and slings. The weight of the two pouches was 1.4 kg. In addition, a large water flask was carried. The leather pouch introduced later, with a shoulder strap, was more practical. The contents were roughly the same; the weight of 3 kg was greater.

In the medical kits for medical NCOs and men, the left pouch held bandaging materials, the right one medicines, including iodine or antiseptic tincture, salicic formalin and alkali eye ointment, various types of tablets, rubber bandages, quick bandages; it weighed 1.6 kg.

The medical kit with shoulder strap was similar.

The medical NCO was also equipped with bandaging materials and a small set of instruments in a leather case, which included scissors, forceps, a thermometer, etc.

The medical canister was equipped with a number of medicines, instruments and bandages, and was usually issued to medical NCOs on the higher staffs.

Every motor vehicle except motorcycles and towing tractors was to carry its own bandage case for immediate first aid in case of injuries from accidents.

The mountain medical kit (Geb.San. Kasten) was carried in appropriate circumstances. It was a cotton bag that was filled by medical officers out of their own supplies and used by small commands in mountain action without medical personnel, carried in one man's pack. It contained quick bandages, packets of large and small bandages, tubes of tablets, frostbite and anti-light salves. It weighed 300 grams.

Every medical officer carried on a shoulder strap or on his saddle, as permanent equipment, an unfolding medical kit with upper and lower sections and a weight of four kilograms. It allowed quick first aid for injuries and wounds. In a metal box, which also served as an insert into the kit, it contained the most important medicines, bandages, metal spirit container with 2 cc injections, needles, tourniquet, etc.

Medical saddlebags for horses, one each on the left and right, were used by mounted units.

Along with this permanent equipment of medical officers, NCOs and men, as well as stretcher bearers, there were also medical boxes.

These medical boxes were among the equipment of troop and medical units with medical materials. Thanks to a practical and visible division of every kit, a comparatively small space held a great number of medicines, bandages and small implements. Each box weighed 50 kg, and they were carried on trucks, or dropped by the paratroops.

The mountain medical boxes, with similar contents, had a greater weight of 79 kg, and were made to be carried by a beast of burden, with weight on both sides. They were formed of two parts attached together, and could be strapped to the sides of a carrying saddle. By detaching the coupling, the double load could be divided into four equal parts, each of which could be carried by one man like a knapsack or backpack.

Medical kits for poison gas treatment were not used.

Medical equipment also included the so-called light kit:

The troop's medical equipment was available to the troop doctor in a battalion or other unit. It held the medical materials that were needed in the first general medical treatment of the troops. This Kit A consisted of five individual boxes and was carried on the medical equipment truck or combat vehicle. Box 1, called the combat box, contained all the medicine, bandages and implements that the troop doctor needed for short-term combat. Boxes 2 through 5 completed the equipment and weighed about 50 kg in all.

In addition, every Kit A of the troops' medical equipment included one backpack filtering device to prepare drinking water from ponds, brooks or non-reliable wells. This device, weighing 19.5 kg, provided 100 to 200 liters of drinking water per hour, depending on the nature of the water.

In the mountain troops, the loads were carried on 25 beasts of burden and three equipment trucks. The animals had 902 kg (Kit K) of medical equipment and 745 kg of foodstuffs to carry.

A Set B of medical supplies was available to the division doctor and formed the first supply of medical material available to the troop and medical units within the division. In addition, the army medical units were equipped with this medical supply set. It consisted of 24 boxes with a total weight of 2700 kg, and was carried on a three-ton truck.

The medical companies were equipped with Set C of medical supplies (dismantled and packed large equipment) for the HV station, platoon or echelon. It consisted of 12 boxes, and was carried on a 1.5-ton truck.

A completion set served to amplify Set C in the medical company. It had as its main contents the equipment for bandaging and gathering stations. With narcotics and equipment for operations, it assured the company's bandaging station crew's ability to perform surgery.

Similar sets were also used by platoons handling slight illnesses, mountain troops, tropical units, army medical parks, hospital platoons and other units.

Every field and military hospital was equipped with two of Set D. An individual Set D consisted of 15 boxes and, with its extensive equipment, guaranteed full care and treatment for all the wounded and sick. A medium truck provided sufficient loading space for this 1500 kg load.

As individual items in addition to the sets of field medical equipment, there were, as already noted, various medical packs, beginning with pocket packs for troop medical officers, with instruments needed for medical care, plus bandaging- and gathering-station implements for operations and treatments of all kinds, and even metal detectors. In addition, specialized medical implements were also available. Additional equipment included field lighting equipment, blood-transfusion devices, operating tables, giant magnets, revival equipment and light and heavy X-ray units. A one-armed oxygen device was also available. It had four attachment points and was carried in a wooden box along with a steel tank holding seven liters of oxygen. For hospitals there was also a large two-armed device with steel tanks holding ten liters. There were also anesthetic, sterilizing and instrument cleaning devices.

Dental field equipment at first consisted of a dental marching kit for urgent cases and six different sets, likewise in crates, including a foot-operated dental drill. Also of importance were the large devices for preparation, such as the sterilizing and detoxifying of dirty or germ-laden water, such as the army drinking water preparer, distilling apparatus and freshwater producer, with a weight of 1200 kg, carried on a 2.5-ton truck.

Extensive and varying field laboratories allowed all kinds of bacteriological investigations and the like. In particular. there were also disinfecting and sterilizing devices.

To operate all the large equipment, generators (for example, for lights, X-ray machines, etc.) were necessary. On a single baseplate they held a power source and a generator, the latter directly coupled to the gasoline engine (air-cooled one-cylinder 1.8 HP motor). They were packed in transportable crates which also held tools and spare parts. The 220 Volt machinery, on a single-axle trailer, was the uniform power source for the greater part of the electrically powered medical equipment at the HV stations and field and military hospitals. All the medical units were supplied with a device that produced enough to meet their great needs. For mountain medical companies there was a generating machine that weighed 23 kg and was a medium load for a beast of burden or could even be carried in the mountains by one man on a back carrier.

Among the medical tents there was, first, the wounded tent (five-piece) used by the medical companies, with room for twenty beds. It could be set up in 20 to 30 minutes by six stretcher bearers, and covered an area of 20 x 7 meters. By adding intermediate parts, it could be given various shapes. It weighed 215 kg, and five tents could be carried on a 2.5-ton truck. The medical companies also had an operating or bandaging tent, capable of being set up by four stretcher bearers in 15 minutes. It covered 7 x 9.4 meters, weighed 171 kg, and was carried along with wounded tents.

Mountain troops had their own tents, which were made so they could be dismantled and carried on beasts of burden. For troops in Africa there were particularly light tents.

Among other tent types there was the wooden tent which was used particularly in the northern theater of war. It consisted of a free-standing round text of the Finnish type for sparsely populated areas in which frequent putting up and taking down were to be avoided because of the chance of damage. The site should be sheltered from the wind. Branches, twigs and snow could be used to provide extra warmth and protection. A small stove inside the tent, set on stones, provided heat.

On a wooden surface, slightly sloping to the center, there was room for twenty sick or wounded men. With an internal diameter of 5.5 meters and an average height of 1.5 meters, it weighed 75 kilograms.

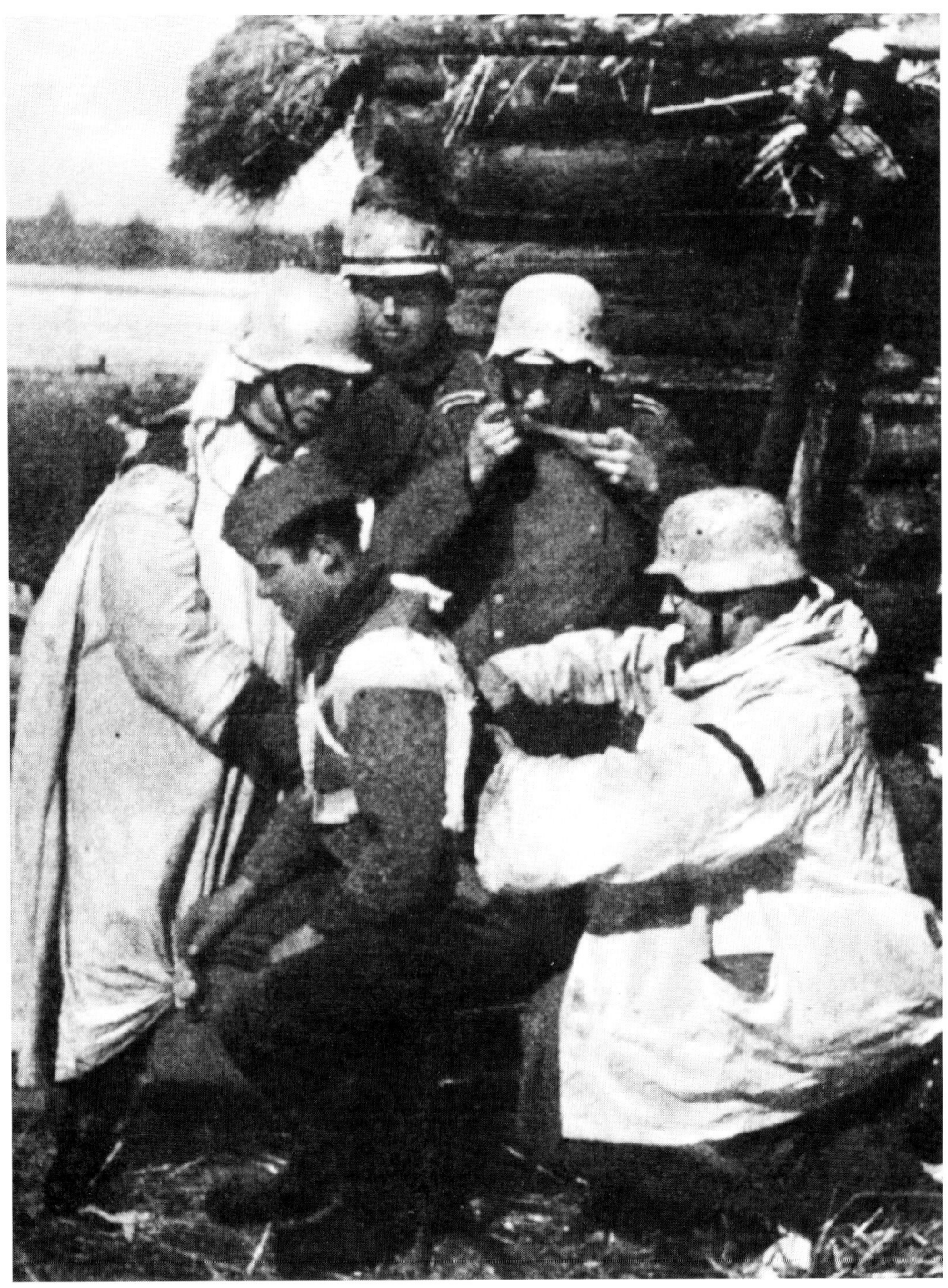
At the troop bandaging station.

Transport Means and Equipment

By all kinds of means of transport, and in all terrains, wounded and sick were to be taken as quickly, safely and comfortably as possible to the appropriate treatment facilities. For this, not only all the means of the medical services were used by the troops, but so was whatever could be improvised to serve this purpose in a pinch. In general, all means of land, water and air transport that brought materials to the front could bring sick and wounded men to the hinterlands on their return trips.

The most urgent task was constantly moving the wounded backward from the front lines. The simplest way to move those who could not walk was the carrying seat, for which the hands of two comrades were folded, left and right, or the man was carried sitting on a horizontal rifle, or more rarely piggyback. Badly wounded men, who had to be carried lying flat, were often brought from the front on blankets or tent canvas, which had to be grasped by four soldiers. This resulted in a major problem—on the one hand, comradeship required helping to bring the man to the troop bandaging station, but on the other, platoons and companies were definitely weakened by the absence, often for a long time, of the carriers. For longer distances, stretcher-bearer companies, often composed of prisoners, were used. Essentially, every wounded man had to make his way back to the troop bandaging station as long as he could still walk.

Transport in the medical corps involved a goodly number of devices that were used more or less often. These included field transport rails, transport hammocks and baskets for rescue and transport from narrow and low spaces, such as in forts.

Most often used were the field carriers made of two equal halves, available in all medical units as their most important transport devices. They could be carried securely in ambulances, medical planes and trains. When extended, their length was 2.4 meters; they weighed 16 kg and could be carried by two men.

Since there were usually not enough field carriers on hand, there were numerous instructions for making carriers out of blankets, or of two uniform jackets with stakes. There was also a holding apparatus for sidecar motorcycles in troop and medical units, weighing 6.3 kg and carrying one lying patient, or a two-wheeled frame for two seated men, weighing 20.3 kg and pulled by two men.

Both types of moving the sick and wounded were utilized by the paratroops.

A one-wheeled carrying device was issued to mountain medical units; it weighed 11.5 kg and allowed the movement of wounded on narrow mountain paths. The device could be folded up and strapped onto backpacks, but was rarely used. For mountain troops there was also the so-called carrying cloth, which was carried in medical officers' and men's packs. It was very light and handy, and consisted of a rectangular sack of watertight material. On each long side there were three handholds attached. The middle of the fabric was closed by a drawstring through hooks and eyes. A wounded or sick man could be carried by six men, each taking one handhold or carrying it by three short stakes or branches passing through the handholds, or it could be carried by two men using two long stakes. The carrying cloth could also be used as a cable container or a sleeping bag. It measured 2 x 0.5 meters when spread out, and weighed only 4 kilograms. The further medical equipment of the mountain troops included steel carriers and cable containers (with cable brakes) to move wounded men (and freight) up and down cables in rocky and icy terrain. With a set of ski attachments (2 kg), carried by stretcher bearers in their packs, four skis could be used as runners and the carrying cloth could be made into a light sled in a few minutes. It was moved by two skiers, who pulled it on lines. There was also a ski-sled device weighing 4.7 kg that could be issued by medical parks on request, likewise to carry one sick or wounded man lying flat. An additional device with raised handholds, guided by two skiers before and behind, was mainly suited to downgrades.

The Akja was especially useful as a sliding device in winter snow or swampy land. It was pulled either by two to four soldiers or by two dogs. On the Arctic front it was also pulled by reindeer. The Akja was made of wood in a boatlike shape, weighed 15 kg, and carried one wounded or sick man lying flat.

At first, an ambulance was still available in the horsedrawn medical companies. In it, four lying or two lying and four sitting wounded or sick could be carried simultaneously. Then it was no longer produced. Best known and most often used by medical companies, field hospitals and motorized ambulance platoons was the Sanitätskraftwagen (Kfz. 31)—generally shortened to "Sanka" (but officially "Sankra"). It could carry four lying, two lying and four sitting, or eight sitting soldiers.

The closed body was heated, had a 20-liter water container, and double main doors at the rear, though it could also be entered through side doors.

Technical data: Load limit to 1200 kg, net weight 2230 kg, width 2.0 meters, height 2.2 meters. The universal chassis for heavy cars was used, with single front and double rear tires.

Ambulances on three-ton chassis—including tracked types—were used as a new design. They allowed the simultaneous transport of nine lying and three sitting wounded or sick. There were also other truck types with closed bodies.

For armored units, the medium Schützenpanzerwagen was rebuilt with special interior details to serve as an ambulance. In addition to its staff, it could hold four lying and two sitting, two lying and six sitting, or twelve sitting patients. The technical data were: Weight 8500 kg, length 5.8 meters, width 2.2 meters, height 2 meters, lightly armored against infantry fire and splinters.

In addition, typical Army omnibuses (seating 16 to 30) were set up as transport vehicles in areas near the front.

To carry large numbers, mainly of severely wounded men, from the field and military hospitals to get further treatment in hospitals back home, hospital trains were established and used more frequently as the war went on. Four-axle express passenger cars were equipped for use in hospital trains. They were already in existence in peacetime. Two-axle railroad cars were also assembled to form hospital trains. Operating rooms, living space, offices, kitchen, supply rooms, heaters or refrigerators completed the trains with the red crosses. They were in excellent condition and staffed by sufficient doctors and medical personnel, including Red Cross nurses. In a single car there was room for up to 30 lying patients. Later, especially in the east, makeshift wounded trains (BVZ) without markings were also used often. They consisted of freight cars with wooden floors and straw, stoves and simple toilets, a field kitchen on a flatcar, and only a few medical personnel. Slightly wounded men helped take care of the badly wounded patients in these cars.

In Russia and the Balkans, even trains with wounded men were not safe from rail and bridge explosions or attacks by partisans.

Although the medical services of the Luftwaffe and Navy are not being dealt with in this volume, yet a few means of transport should be noted, as they were of particular service to Army wounded. These included several types of Luftwaffe aircraft that were not intended for combat use. They were as follows:

The Fieseler "Storch" (F 1/156 C-2), actually a 2- to 3-seat communication and observation plane. Its technical data were: wingspan 14.25 meters, length 9.90 m, maximum take-off weight 1325 kg, top speed 175 kph, range 380 km, one-man crew. This plane, available only in very limited numbers, was used as an ambulance plane for transport in

25

rough country (mountains, trackless areas), and could carry two badly wounded men lying flat.

The Junkers Ju 53, popularly known as "Aunt Ju" and plentiful, was a very robust, slow but reliable medium-range transport plane. It had a wingspan of 29.20 meters, length 18.90 m, take-off weight 11,020 kg, cruising speed 257 kph, range 1500 km, three engines, three-man crew.

Used as an ambulance plane, it bore red crosses on its fuselage and wings. The plane could normally carry 18 slightly wounded men or 13 stretchers with seriously wounded men, plus attendants. Used since the war began, the Ju 52—as long as it could manage to land at all—was nearly indispensible for quick and safe transport of the wounded. It worked out that practically every Ju 52 that brought freight to the front took wounded men on its return flight.

The Me 323 "Gigant," then the world's largest land plane, was used in small numbers as of 1942 as a gigantic large-capacity transport plane. Wingspan 55 meters, length 28.10 m, six engines, ten landing wheels, five-man crew. The big transport was loaded from the front through its double bow doors. Its loading capacity was one 88 mm gun with its towing tractor, or 130 fully equipped soldiers, etc. It could carry up to 150 sitting or 60 lying wounded or sick men.

One great disadvantage of this plane was its ponderousness and vulnerability, which meant that it usually had to fly close to the ground.

The Navy set up its own hospital ships for care of the wounded.

They enjoyed the protection of various Hague and Geneva conventions and were recognized by the warring nations. Yet there were many details to note, beginning with white paint bearing red crosses to identify the prescribed medical personnel. These time-honored agreements dated from 1907 and were linked, among the signatory nations, with a laborious process of announcement and acknowledgment that went on for months. A hospital ship that was fully unarmed was also guaranteed protection for its safety.

The fast course of events in modern warfare outran such formalities and led to makeshift solutions (see wounded transports, below).

Hospital ships with up to 600 beds were, almost without exception, merchant ships that had been modified for their purpose. The large hospital ships displacing 10,000 to 15,000 BRT—unlike the smaller ones of 1000 to 3000 BRT, with 250 to 300 beds—with a full staff of doctors, medical personnel and Red Cross nurses, equaled large-scale hospitals on land in terms of personnel.

At the time of mobilization in 1939, four large and two small hospital ships were available. They took on their importance only as of 1941, when the war moved into the Mediterranean, Aegean and Adriatic areas with the campaigns in Crete, Africa, and finally Italy. Here, for example, during the Allied invasion of Italy, on an open beach near Porto d'Ascoli at a sixty-meter pier built by engineers, some 5500 men, most of them seriously wounded, were taken aboard hospital ships and disembarked at Venice. While the German hospital ships were mostly undisturbed by the British and Americans, the situation was different when the eastern campaign began. From the start, the Soviet Union did not recognize any German hospital ships. This was stated shortly after the Russian campaign began on July 17, 1941 in a note in which they accused the German government of "systematic and treacherous violations of international treaties and conventions."

Thus in the last months of World War II, German hospital ships still became the victims of Soviet attacks.

At first, though, since the main combat took place in the interior of the continent, the use of hospital ships was limited to the Norwegian area, where they had been used since the beginning of the Norwegian campaign in 1940. Here they lay at anchor in the Norwegian Neidenfjord from 1941 on, forming a sort of stationary hospital for the troops on the Arctic front. The main task of the hospital ships, eight more of which were in service at the beginning of 1945, was to make voyages into the Baltic Sea in the last months and weeks of the war. Thus some 155,000 wounded and refugees could be rescued from the attacks of the Soviets. Of the total of 35 hospital ships in service, seven large and twelve small ones were knocked out of service during the war. Three of the ten large ships, and ten of the twenty-five small ones, were sunk by mines, torpedoes or bombs. Only the small hospital ship with the appropriate name "Glückauf" was in service during the entire war.

As replacements or additions to the fleet of hospital ships, more and more so-called wounded transporters saw service. All of them came from civilian shipping.

These ships, introduced by the Navy for the eastern campaign as of mid-1944, were not equipped like hospital ships but did have a medical unit on board. They deliberately avoided any external markings, had no international protection, and were armed with Flak guns. About their service, it was stated on September 26, 1944: "The wounded transporter serves exclusively for the mass transport of wounded on the ocean. The inner conduct on board, according to service instructions, is based on the conduct on hospital ships."

In the course of evacuating eastern German areas, 148,000 wounded, some of them in the last days of the war, were moved by these transporters. Eight of the 36 wounded transporters were lost.

The Army Mountain Medical School

Among the training centers for medical officers and men, this school deserves special mention because of its special features.

The union with Austria in 1938 made it necessary to establish a training center for mountain medical service within the XVIII. Mountain Army Corps. In April 1939 the Corps-Gebirgssanitätsschule began its training activities at the "Edelweiss-Kaserne" in St. Johann in Tirol. Here 180 medical NCOs were trained for Army mountain medical service, and when the war began on September 1, 1939 they were available to the mountain troops and prepared in terms of training and equipment. The Mountain Medical Replacement Unit 18 in Saalfelden, originally with two companies in St. Johann, then took over this training.

In the winter of 1940-41, two mountain medical companies were formed at Lofer to serve the 5th Mountain Division according to the newest knowledge and experience; they served well on all fronts, including airborne duty in Crete, where one of them was landed. Left on their own, they were able to treat all the wounded in the decisive combat. More and more was asked of the mountain troops, of whom more and more were established.

Plans for action in the Caucasus were being made; the right moment had come for the Army High Command to suggest an order for the establishment of a mountain medical school, and within a week it was so ordered. The responsible General Command XVIII in Salzburg was put in charge of this organization. All previous experience and tests in terms of personnel and materials would and could now find their application. Down to the details of filling positions, getting all the required equipment and making some of the instructional plans—all was prepared by the office of the Medical Officer of the Army High Mountain School at Fulpmes im Stubaital. A part of the medical staff was included in the establishment staff of the Army Mountain Medical School. St. Johann in Tirol was to be the so-called peacetime location of the school, meaning that its existence after the war was also envisioned; it was to remain in existence with all its facilities.

The Army Mountain Medical School was divided into:

Command staff (commander, adjutant and appropriate colleagues), officer in the staff for organization and training, plus an intelligence echelon and an experiment unit. Subordinate were the instructional groups with two teaching inspections, the research group and the teaching company with beast-of-burden and dog echelons. Each of these teaching inspections was led by an inspection chief. It had six instructors, several other NCOs and vehicles. Its task was carrying out the training courses, which lasted three weeks as a rule. (One week of theory or instruction at the school and two weeks of training in the mountains, in every season, at huts all over the Alpine area.) Participants were mostly higher medical NCOs and all those medical officers, including the division doctors, who were serving with mountain and Jäger divisions. There were also courses of study for the police and the so-called mountain rescue service of the Army. Members of allied nations also took the courses. In all, more than 6000 men were sent there and trained, not counting those who were detailed to shorter commands.

In 1943 and 1944 the "HGSS" set up five more inspections, to which army doctors whose units were in action at mountain fronts were assigned on order. They were to take courses of study directly on the front or in division sectors, for the medical personnel of the troops who lacked mountain training were not sufficiently capable of doing their tasks.

After the defeat of Rommel's army in North Africa and the constant advance of the Allies from southern Italy, a conference between the commander of Army Group South and the commander of the "HGSS" in 1943 resulted in the opening of another school in the Grödner Valley in South Tyrol, in Plan, above Wolkenstein. The positions in the Apennines were endangered, because half a platoon of a company had to be used to evacuate one wounded man, giving the enemy a chance to break through the main battle line. This school at Plan was also fully occupied to the end of the war.

The so-called Mountain Rescue Service was also linked with the Mountain Medical School and took part in its establishment. All through the Alpine area, appropriate offices were set up. Its personnel came from the members of the mountain patrol in Bavaria and the mountain rescue service of the Alpenverein in Austria, who either had not been drafted or were serving in the homeland. They were taken into service and some of their leaders drafted into the "HGSS." These offices were supplied with the usual rescue equipment, including modern types. Thus it came about that, when the war ended, rescue stations were available and ready for immediate service everywhere, and mountain tourism could benefit from them again.

Again and again, training had to deal with new situations, special instructional plans had to be drawn up. They included everything that concerned mountain service in any season and had to be developed specifically in terms of mountain techniques, including the special conditions of treating wounded and sick in the mountains. The teachers of the courses of study were in part Army mountain guides, and some were guides from the Alpenverain. All of them were detailed to teach at the Army High Mountain School in Fulpmes in order to maintain or attain a high level of instruction. Independent leadership of a rescue troop was a prerequisite, and it included thorough training, especially as rescue situations often turned out to be more difficult than had been foreseen in theory. Thus it is easy to understand that the mountain rescue equipment and its absolute suitability were paramount; on it, along with the knowledge of the rescuers, help and success depended. When the mountain troops were established with one brigade in October 1936, there were only two devices for the mountain medical service: the so-called mountain patrol ski attachment and the Gramminger cable seat with a special brake hook. The army stretcher, consisting of two equal parts that could be combined, was unsuitable for mountain use in that form, but at first there was nothing else. This, among other places, was also the case with the medical unit in Mittenwald.

Here the important and vital work of the experimental department of the Army Mountain Medical School at St. Johann in Tirol began. The leader of this department, Dr. Rometsch, brought the steel cable device, originated and developed by him, from his front service with the 4th Mountain Division. The use of a steel cable in Alpine rescue service was absolutely new at that time. The steel cable, which could be of any length, was braked in the simplest way by wrapping it around a fixed wooden post. Now came the opportunity to complete this device and test it under all conditions. With the assistance of his colleagues, Dr. Mariner and Dipl.-Ing. Schurich, the device was now developed further, also in view of its versatility of use as a cableway as opposed to a hanging cable, but especially for winching down high, inaccessible rock faces.

Inspired by the particular position on the so-called "Stiegler carrier" which was already used in World War I, the Army patient carrier had to be replaced in terms of its possibilities of position. The patient was to be translated in a crouching position, with legs drawn up, and somewhat relaxed. A steel frame in rocker shape was developed as a resting or transporting possibility for the wounded. This frame only needed to be set on the single wheel instead of the field carrier. This was done in two types of support, in front for use as a wheelbarrow or in the middle as before, guided by two helpers. But the frame itself was also suitable for being slid sledlike over slopes and light gravel.

The patient-carrier sled device had also proved itself, especially when used with two spar handholds. It could be moved quickly on a downgrade, at which time it was necessary for the two helpers to wear short skis themselves. It could also be hooked up in tandem and pulled by dogs, mules, horses or motor vehicles. This was done particularly on the Arctic front. There the natives used the so-called Akja, which was their special vehicle for all purposes.

Now the question arose as to whether these Akjas could also be used in the mountains. Guiding them brought on difficulties in terms of their weight and mass. The Akja was now divided into two halves both longitudinally and transversely. In the longitudinal form, a helper could fasten one end to his backpack while the other trailed along behind; in the transverse form, each half could be attached to a pack without problems.

The research group dealt with all the questions of mountain medicine in a broad sense, on a scientific basis. The problems for the altitude-physiological department developed from the question: "How does the soldier behave in the high mountains, and how is his functioning influenced in terms of altitude, temperature, snow, sunshine and, particularly, high bodily strain. How successful is adaptation, how can one shorten it, keep it constant, etc." Experimental groups at the school were methodically tested and observed under appropriate conditions. Scientists from several universities participated. For example, a physiologist from the Luftwaffe was always detailed to the research group in order to test for better altitude acceptance among pilots under mountain conditions. Pilots were gathered for courses of study, in order to accustom themselves to the Oberwalder Hut at 3000-meter altitude.

The research of the chemical-physiological group covered questions of nourishment, dry food, preservation, etc., as well as questions of clothing, and tests were carried out under high mountain conditions. One scientists was a pharmacologist and examined the different digestive conditions. Several scientific works of the "HGSS" were published, and scientists could continue their academic training at the school.

In 1943 a mountain physiological conference was held there.

In the same year, a chain-motorcycle unit was formed there in its own building, to transport materials over the glacier, and an extension of the Oberwalder Hut was built in which a high-altitude physiological laboratory was established. It functioned in the same way as other such institutions in other countries. The instructional company had a beginning strength of some 80 men and was the school's introductory and experimental troop. Connected to it were the motor vehicle unit and a canine unit. The latter deserves special mention here, as it was planned for the special training of avalanche dogs. Historically preserved accounts and advice on the rescue of avalanche victims by St. Bernard dogs at the St. Bernard Pass made it seem possible to train and use dogs again for avalanche rescue. These tests led to astounding results. The dogs almost always found test persons in dug-in angled shafts, often in 3 to 4 meters of snow. According to specific methods, the dogs were now used and trained according to plan. In the summer they were kept in igloos of snow at the Oberwalder Hut, in order to keep them in snow and ice as much as possible all year. The avalanche rescue dog unit was soon renowned all over the Alpine country and often called on for help.

The school collapsed in the crush of events at the end of the war and was used as a hospital for several months.

The remaining medical officers and personnel, supported by volunteer helpers, devoted all their efforts to wounded men from hospital trains which had been left on the rails at St. Johann.

Those who died in this hospital found their last resting place in the military cemetery in St. Johann.

Oberstabsarzt Dr. Schaefer

Russian prisoners help bring in a wounded man.

Icy Russia and Hot Africa

After the heavy losses in the first half-year of the Russian campaign, the German Eastern Army once again had to survive serious losses against an enemy with whom nobody had reckoned—"General Winter." The first war winter of 1941-42 was to be Russia's coldest and snowiest in 140 years. At times the thermometer dropped to -30 degrees and farther (in January, at times, to -40), and the show's height rose to one meter. The German soldier was exposed to this winter almost defenseless; for him there were scarcely any warm lodgings, but rather combat lasting days and nights in biting cold. At the highest command level, it was thought that the campaign would take about four months, so that nobody prepared for the cold weather. Despite the threatening winter, the further advance, particularly against Moscow, was ordered, instead of establishing fixed winter quarters. The whole Eastern Army—unlike the Soviet Army—was not at all dressed or equipped for a winter war.

It was not correct that winter clothing was in storage and could not be delivered to the front at the right time. A suitable winter uniform was only issued as of the winter of 1943-44.

So in the beginning the German soldiers wore their thin cloth coats, their folding-down Schiffchen caps, earmuffs, a face mask, gloves, and boots whose hobnails made them all the colder. As underwear they wore a thin woolen vest and a body belt (and long underpants in any case). But that was all (other than heavy coats and such for sentries, drivers, etc.). A great call for donations of winter clothing and equipment (especially skis and sleds) in the Reich was answered eagerly and generously, to be sure, but these things arrived at the front much too late and—hardly suitable for the troops—could scarcely be used. It was unavoidable that the fighting forces suffered more and more frostbite, which soon grew to a frightful extent and exceeded the number of wounded. Statistics offer a conception of this:

In the 122th Infantry Division, which fought southeast of Moscow that winter, every regiment had over 400 casualties on account of freezing alone. In all, the Eastern Army had 14,357 serious, 62,000 medium and 36,270 slight cases of freezing in the winter months, through February 20, 1942. While most slight cases could stay with the troops, all the others had to be treated in hospitals, and serious cases often required amputation. It should not be forgotten that in this and the following winter, all the wounded also had to suffer pain and misery on account of the coldness and snow as well.

Oberfeldarzt Dr. Dr. H. Fischer wrote in No. 8 of the Military Medical Journal in 1981, among other things:

During the winter combat in the east in 1941-42, with their tremendous physical and spiritual burdens, regular treatment of the wounded was no longer possible in many places. The organization broke down and one had to try through constant improvisation to master the difficulties. Troop doctors and medical units were left on their own, usually overworked, and often at the end of their powers. Merciless combat and icy temperatures demanded countless sacrifices. Every limitation of movement could result in death by freezing. For bodily weakened wounded men whose feet, boots and all, formed blocks of ice, all concepts of wound treatment carried out 'lege artis' were useless. Long-untreated shot wounds in connection with undercooling and freezing led to complications to an extent never before known."

On the other hand, the North African theater of war had its own extremes. At first, no medical services with tropical experience were available. In the instruction book for medical NCOs, only seven pages were devoted to the most important tropical diseases, such as malaria, sleeping sickness, amebic dysentery, Maltese fever, etc., and general rules took up only half a page. But many typical tropical problems resulted from constant climatic changes with very hot days and cold nights, dehydration, unvaried plain food, lack of fresh provisions, housing only in tents for lack of buildings, etc. When wounded men remained without treatment for a long time, wound infections generally developed and could prove fatal. All the soldiers knew that atabrine was to be taken daily to avoid malaria.

This theater of war had one advantage: in warfare that was waged chivalrously by both sides, the Red Cross was respected and the sick and wounded were treated considerately.

Yet throughout the war, the troops were spared epidemics and other serious diseases that had wiped out entire armies in earlier times, including typhus infections carried by lice. Of course, as the eastern campaign went on, the entire army at the front was thoroughly overrun by lice in the end. In quiet times, the soldiers tried to protect themselves by delousing their uniforms, and in camps the medical units helped with saunas and delousing stations; the sanitary facilities did the same, and their were also mobile delousing stations.

The Army Physician reported that from the beginning of the eastern campaign in mid-1941 to mid-1942, the total number of typhus cases in the Eastern Army was 32,718, with 3,196 deaths. From September 1943 to May 1945, there were many thousand cases; exact statistics are not available.

At the focal point of the battle against infectious diseases were the field bacteriological laboratories, which made all necessary investigations possible. Army pharmacists also contributed decisively, through strict watchfulness, timely and appropriate distribution of medicines, to preventing the spread of such diseases as malaria, Wollyn fever, etc. Thus the number of such cases remained so low that one could never speak of epidemics.

Good knowledge of epidemeology and simple but effective hygienic measures maintained the health of the troops despite all the severe physical and psychological strains, and also fought against disease in the civilian populations.

It was remarkable how the soldiers, most of whom came from cities, soon learned to handle all the hardships of war and strengthened themselves more and more against its pressures and deprivations.

Medical Corps in Action

Bandaging Stations of the 254th Infantry Division in the French Campaign, 1940

On the advance route between Furnes and Bergues, the medical columns hurried after the combat units of their divisions. The final combat would be around Dunkirk!

Wedged in between artillery and heavy trucks, several vehicles with red crosses pushed forward; they were the motorized part of the horsedrawn Medical Company 1 of the 254th Infantry Division.

The French border was now behind them. Then the jam loosened up and the men knew they would soon reach the site for the ordered main bandaging station. The company's motorcycle messengers appeared at a crossroads and guided the few trucks into a small village. The major combat could be seen ahead of them. Plumes of smoke rose before their staring eyes from the burned-out houses. Only the staff doctor and the company chief—who had worked their way up through the ranks in World War I—thought about the old battlefields to the west. "Right turn! Halt! Dismount!" Several troops went out to reconnoiter—looking for the hospital or the school. No hospital, but the school was there, very small, but undamaged. Several slightly damaged houses and a big meadow nearby. The Oberarzt, leader of Platoon II, was followed by two men with the signs: San.Kp. HV-Platz, Aufnahme, Anfahrt, Abfahrt, Schreibstube (Medical Co., HV Station, Reception, Entry, Exit, Writing Room). As practiced a hundred times and learned from experience in minor actions, the medical soldiers of Platoon II brought in the equipment and set it up in the empty rooms. As in a disturbed anthill—the chief thought. But soon the confusion decreased and order prevailed again.

Even before the report to Division IV b: "HV Station in X ready for action!" reached the division doctor, the first wounded were there, and action had begun. Our "drive-it-yourself" bicycle echelon of Platoon I, reported their arrival. The stretcher bearers filled rooms with straw piles to hold "untreated" and "treated." Soon after that, good news arrived. The horsedrawn forces of Platoon III, writing room, paymaster, field kitchen and supplies, had reached the scene already—who knows how!

The chief had informed himself about the HV station of the next company and located a parking place for the vehicles. The misery of the retreating enemy forces showed in the chaos of the retreat route. The heaps of equipment of all kinds, tipped-over wagons, dead horses, abandoned trucks, and abandoned weapons bordered the roads for kilometers. Signs to direct the ambulances were put up at crossroads.

Returning to the HV station, "the Old Man" passed out captured British map material—splendidly drawn on linen, a valuable prize for messengers, ambulance drivers and leaders. In addition, he had found two British ambulances, had them towed in and made ready for use, a great gain in terms of the company's readiness. Too bad they couldn't hide them from the division. The arriving ambulances of the ambulance platoon brought the first information on the locations of the troop bandaging stations and battalion command posts.

Things were crowded at admission and in the operating room. The stream of arrivals kept on growing. According to the Oberarzt's reports, the surgeons were already working in two groups, with internists and dentists assisting. The Oberapotheker and his pharmacy helpers had their hands full bringing the medical materials in. The medical corporal assigned to sterilizing received help from Platoon III. Many badly wounded men arrived and required the best and quickest work from the surgeons and medics. All the badly wounded men already treated were doing well. Except for one man who died while being brought in, there were no fatalities.

Between the treated and untreated patients, the stretcher bearers went from litter to litter. Many who had been pastors in civilian life not only met the physical needs, bringing tea and urine bottles, but also cared for those who faced the hereafter, giving them faith, consolation and confidence, and took their last messages to the folks back home. The battle with death was extremely difficult.

The third platoon had to expand the admission area. The company chief himself took over the initial treatment of the arriving badly wounded men, checking their bandages, giving injections, setting up the order of operations.

Once again the stretcher bearers unloaded an arriving ambulance. The driver's aide gestured for caution! At first, several slightly wounded man clambered out. Then a carrier was carefully set on the ground. An ashen face looked out of a shapeless mass of bandages. No signs of life, no groaning! Suddenly all were silent with shared sorrow. But he was still alive.

He was a Panzerman with both arms smashed, splinter wounds on the torn left side of his face. He was in deep shock. "Call the Oberarzt; another surgeon should take his place at the operation!"

Conference between chief and first surgeon. Both decided: Rest first. Scarcely any hope. Four badly wounded men were still waiting for treatment urgently needed for survival. So the unconscious dying man was taken to a quiet place, namely the morgue room in a section of the cellar.

Otherwise the fury of the battle was heard and seen everywhere, with the firing of distant guns, single airplanes attacking, the growl of tank engines, and bursts of fire.

The night went on. For a long time, everything had been equipped with emergency lighting and darkened. The property NCO had a mountain of personal possessions with field post numbers, gas masks and weapons. Among the surgeons and the second platoon, any chance of relief had become impossible. The readiness of the medical personnel did their best to preserve human feelings.

As usual, drivers and patients brought wild rumors from the front in the outskirts of Dunkirk, for example, that dive-bombers tried in vain to shatter the strong forts. Toward noon of the second day, the arrivals began to decrease. Doctors and medics fell onto their straw piles. In the free time, the rooms were cleaned, heaps of bloody bandages and scraps of uniforms were burned.

Coffins and crosses made on the spot were ready for the burial place. The dead were gathered for a short burial service. Then a stretcher bearer rushed up: "Herr Stabsarzt, one of the dead is alive!" This hit the doctor's conscience hard: the dying Panzerman lying in the cellar! Yes, he was still alive! A sigh of relief overcame the shock. Immediate careful preparation and operation. Well treated, he was taken to the field hospital and was able to survive. One of the most instructive experiences for the later large-scale combat in the east had been gained unwillingly by the surgery group and the whole second platoon: wounded men in deep shock need a long rest first.

Again the number of arrivals grew beyond the possibility of immediate care. The wounded men were so wet they dripped. Fighting in the flood plains beside the roads had caused the most extreme exhaustion. Lying under water, the barbed-wire fences of the cow pastures could not be seen, and the soldiers remained hanging on them in the dark, in danger of drowning, and injured themselves even more. The roadway was under the heaviest defensive fire from men who fought desperately, brave enemy defenders.

35

In the night, the companies received orders to make use of medical dogs. One battalion had to remove some trees under the defensive fire of the enemy.

A dog trainer went with the medical dog "Arno," the company's friend, through the thick brush, under constant enemy fire, to find several dead and badly wounded men who could be brought out.—The dog later received special recognition from the Military Medical Dog School in Berlin, and the medical corporal received the company's first Iron Cross Grade II.

During this major action, the division's medical units did a special deed. To care for wounded enemies—whose numbers were too great for care at the HV stations—a surgical group was detailed to the field hospital, which quickly treated some 800 wounded British soldiers simultaneously with the German wounded.

On the third day there was a lull. The arrival of wounded men decreased slowly. Ambulance halting places were set up ahead, for the troops had reached Dunkirk itself; one of our regiments had captured the northern edge of town.

The first preparations for a future move of the company began already. Superfluous instruments, cleaned and sterilized, were packed into their shipping cases, and some of the supplies of bandages, medicine and operating clothes were packed up.

Roll call for the company. The little field blacksmith's shop put out its fire. The "writing war" was finished, with all its reports, sketch maps of positions and burial places, arrival and departure records of wounded and sick, strength reports, reports to IV about losses of horses, records of received commands—finished.

On the next day the company moved through Dunkirk. On the beach at Malo les Bains, long landing stages reached far into the sea. Hundreds of vehicles were left side by side, with beams laid over them. Over them, the beaten British had climbed to their ships. Over the harbor, sky-high black clouds rose from the big, burning gasoline tanks. Near Gravelines, beside the road, lay the monsters—the heaviest long-range guns.

Then came days of rest in Guisnes, and from Cap Gris Nez the British coast could be seen, a white line along the horizon, with the high chalk cliffs of Dover.

Oberfeldarzt d.R. Cr. W.

Short Report of the Medical Company of the 205th Infantry Division

The Medical Company 205 was formed from the Lw. Medical Company 14 (cadre from Donaueschingen). Its first bandaging stations were in Freiburg and Emmendingen. When the division was transferred, it was domiciled in the Immendingen area, and later in the Münsingen-Mehrstetten area. Its main task was training medical personnel after exchanging all its older men.

As a result of the fast advance of the motorized parts of the army in the western campaign of 1940, the division, being horsedrawn, was spared major combat. Fortunately, the medical soldiers' main task was chiefly the treatment of sick soldiers, and the care of the French civilian population, which was bereft of doctors.

After going on furlough, the division was transferred to the Nantes-Vanes-St. Anne d'Auray area. In this area it took over the local hospitals and set up HV stations. It treated all the Wehrmacht units that were in action on the Atlantic Wall.

At the end of January 1942, it was sent by rail to Vitebsk and had its first contact with the Russian winter. Sanitary and hygienic conditions in its housing were incredibly primitive. Its first large HV station was in Belyayevo, with a later "branch office" in Velich, where it received many wounded, including General

Richter. Further action included HV stations in the area of Velikiye Luki, Spaspaladi, Nedomerki, Nassva, Lobno, Minikino, Senkova, Polozk, Svedlichitche and Frauenburg.

In the autumn of 1943, Medical Company 205 was divided into Med. Co. 1/205 (horsedrawn) and Med. Co. 2/205 (mot), with remnants of a Sudeten German and Saxon medical company. In July 1944, Med. Co. 1/205 left the division and served elsewhere in the corps. Med. Co. 2/205 was captured by the Russians along with the division.

From a report of Stabsarzt Dr. van de Loo, then company chief, these data can be noted: Ten HV stations were set up, three local hospitals, one patient gathering area, four advanced motorized surgical groups. In the report period from 2/10/1942 to 5/31/1943, 16,769 wounded and sick known by name, plus 5,900 wounded not known by name, from the combat around Velich, Belyayevo and Velikiye-Luki were treated.

According to information from the then personnel officer on the division staff, the total losses of the division in the eastern campaign were about 34,000 men, of whom one third were killed and two thirds wounded. It can be presumed that, out of the number of wounded, another 15% died of serious wounds, so that the number of dead can be estimated at 16,000.

Within this framework, it is only possible to estimate the achievements of the medical personnel (doctors, NCOs and men). Anyone who did not experience it himself can scarcely imagine with what difficulties they had to contend: the most primitive housing for bandaging and operating rooms, medical duties in far below normal peacetime conditions, almost criminal asepsis (bandages and operations), unbroken work during major combat action, to the point of total physical and psychological exhaustion, sometimes under enemy fire, in intense cold and constant disgust with filth and mud.

The transport of the wounded went on at times under conditions that could hardly be endured. Mud and ice made ambulances break down, plus hours-long trips through partisan areas, often under fire. The service of the brave men of the small ambulance platoon, under the command of Hauptmann Peter, deserves special mention. In all service, improvisation, a sense of duty, and the will to keep going brought out personal strengths that the men had never before known. The excellent service to dental patients under the most primitive conditions was provided by the dentists, Dr. Berberich and Dr. Fischer.

For lack of space, it is impossible to name all of those who deserve recognition. One doctor shall represent them—Stabsarzt Dr. Katz, whose outstanding personal, professional and physical performance set an example for all, and who was one of the very few medical officers of the Army Group North to be decorated with the "German Cross in Silver."

With the Airborne Assault Regiment in Crete in 1941

With the landing of the Airborne Assault Regiment (known as Group West during the combat), the regiment's medical corpsmen parachuted into enemy fire or landed in gliders. In the troops under the command of the regimental doctor, Oberstabsarzt Dr. Neumann, divided by battalion (I-IV) as medical echelons, each had five medical officers, 15 medical NCOs and 20 stretcher bearers. The 3rd Company of Paratroop Medical Unit 7, under Oberarzt Dr. Dietzel, was detailed to strengthen the medical services.

A particular stroke of bad luck at the beginning was that containers of medical supplies and equipment were dropped too late, and some landed among the enemy. Soon more and more wounded came in, some alone despite serious wounds, some accompanied by comrades, to the first temporary bandaging station in a house in Tavronitis, where 171 wounded were treated on the first day. Makeshift tents made of parachutes were also set up to house the patients. The losses were heavy; among the fatalities of the third battalion alone were three medical officers.

Transport to the Greek mainland for further treatment was urgent. Thus on the very second day, 35 badly wounded men were taken back on a returning Ju 52 from the Malemes airfield, which was still under enemy shell fire. The regular transport could begin as of May 24. From the airborne hospital set up by the 3rd Medical Company, a total of 1630 wounded men could be treated and sent away by air on May 26-31, for a total of 3400 German wounded and all the British wounded.

Here is one episode:

Among the other wounded a paratrooper was brought in with a severe wound in the left armpit. His makeshift bandage was thoroughly soaked with blood. The bleeding could not be stopped.

Oberarzt Dr. Weizel had to make a hard decision. If he removed the bandage, the bleeding would become even stronger. The wounded man would not survive that. But a complete staunching of the bleeding was not possible with the available means. The only thing that could still save this paratrooper was an immediate blood transfusion. The wounded man was laid flat on the ground. Dr. Weizel added thick layers of cotton wool and gauze to the old bandage, with strips around the chest and shoulder to make it as tight as possible. It looked almost as if that was stopping the bleeding, but then this bandage also turned blood-red.

Immediately after the decision had been made, two medics had been sent to bring the transfusion device. When they returned, gasping under the heavy backpack, it was almost too late. The Oberarzt had already determined the wounded man's blood type. Dr. Weizel, who had the same type, immediately decided to be the donor himself.

He sat down with his back against a tree. Two of his medics put the tourniquet on and inserted the needle. The device worked, the container filled. Then it was reversed, and the doctor's blood flowed into the veins of the wounded man, who was almost bled dry. The man, who was unconscious, came to and asked for a drink. The improbable had happened! He was wrapped in blankets and taken to the hospital. There he was operated on immediately. They were able to tie off and mend the damaged blood vessels.

"Straightening the Front" with the 112th Infantry Division, and the 1st Medical Company, in the Winter of 1941-42 in Russia

The winter had come, with frost that made the roads firm. The wheels rolled over the frozen ground, but the food did not arrive. A cutting wind blew. Earmuffs were on hand, the only piece of winter clothing that had arrived to date.

The division was in contact with the enemy again. That meant for us: set up bandaging stations, treat and transport the wounded. We set things up in a couple of wretched huts. An old woman offered cooked potatoes; we could dig in. Why tighten the belt more and go hungry as long as there were such hospitable people in Russia.

The weather changed, the snow melted and water dripped from the roofs. The vehicles were standing in the mud again. Questions plagued us. Could we stand much more of this kind of warfare? Without regular supplies? Without winter clothing? Rough days were before us. We sensed it and wondered: Is there any purpose to advancing farther and farther to the east?

The division was in battle and suffered heavy losses. All the rooms in the school that we had occupied were full. Once again an overcrowded bandaging station! Suffering faces stared at us; complaining and begging or silent and detached, the wounded lay on the straw. Only at night did a groan resound through the room now and then. The easier hours were long since over.

We doctors and medical soldiers saw what we thought was the greatest misery in this war. Fear and suffering were concentrated around us. Sometimes it almost seemed as if someone wanted to hold us responsible for all this misery. We did what we could.

The division faced fresh Siberian regiments. The right flank was open, and it would not have surprised us if Mongolian faces had suddenly appeared in the doorways. It sounded ridiculous when we read in the arriving newspapers what the "Reich Press Chief" had said a few weeks ago: "The military decision in the eastern campaign has already been made!" At home they must believe that the war had all but ended victoriously. But we felt that the worst hours were still to come.

The arrival of wounded men did not let up. The fighting strength of the infantry had dropped to about fifty men per company. The lack of winter clothing became more and more noticeable. It snowed again, and the frost grew heavier. The coldness penetrated to our bones. Our noses and ears turned white and we began to rub them so they wouldn't fall off.

The enemy attacked again with strong forces. The division had to form a defensive front. The HV station was fully occupied again. The number of wounded arriving grew ever greater. We had to treat more than 500. Means of transporting them out were not available. Our activity consisted mainly of bringing food and straw, treating and caring for the wounded. Thankful eyes looked at us. It was also our job to strengthen their confidence and convince them that too-hasty transport would only increase their suffering. Understanding, they nodded their bandaged heads.

Wounded who arrived spoke of the superior numbers of the enemy, of the ineffectiveness of our own weapons. The situation was serious, critical, there was no doubt of that. The pressure of the enemy increased.

"Get ready to move out immediately. Load wounded into empty columns." This order did not surprise us.

It had grown dark when we left the village. We fought our way through snowdrifts. Ravens and crows accompanied us, they smelled carrion. The sky glowed red. Detonations rang through the night. A rush to the rear began. The severe cold and the high losses forced the German division to retreat.

The operating groups with the surgeons remained at work. The men of the stretcher-bearer platoon were among the last who saved themselves from the enemy. Don't leave any wounded behind, was the word. They were brought along on sleds. That meant that we threw all our unnecessary equipment in the ditches.

On the road there was wild confusion. One saw emblems of the most varied divisions and service arms. Tank crews came along on native sleds; their tanks had run out of gas, or they were left somewhere, shot up or burned out. At bridges and crossroads there were crowds. There was screaming, complaining and cursing. Cars were stuck in ditches, tanks were burning, smoke rose to the heavens. "But that cannot disturb a seaman," rang out at the same time from a radio that was still intact. Sometimes one got the impression that it would be better to go back than to go ahead. It seemed as if even the horses knew what was going on. One soldier sang, "Long is the road back to the Fatherland," (the German version of "Pack up your troubles in your old kit-bag").

One suspected that the retreat was supposed to stop at the Oka river. There a defensive line was supposed to be formed; divisions equipped with winter clothes were supposed to be there, ready to relieve us, so it was said. A lot was said—and hoped.

The Wehrmacht report brought only news of "local combat action," of "straightening the front" and "shortening the front as a result of moving into winter quarters." At home they had no idea what it was like on the front. The enemy was hard on our heels. Men talked of Cossacks who swung their sabers and split skulls open. Wounded men with saber cuts had arrived at the main bandaging station. So it must be true.

The enemy attacked again. His pressure kept getting stronger; in the middle of the division's sector he had broken into our positions. What was waiting for us? The Oka position was to be held under any conditions, it was said. There the news was heard that the enemy had already crossed the river. Could we get out of this hell? "Sunday morning—without worries," said the man on the radio, but it was easy for him to talk. We, on the other hand, were witnesses of a drama known only to those who were actually living it. The seriousness of the situation was no longer disguised. The tension grew, the next hours had to bring a solution.

The 29th of December was a critical day, but also a day of confirmation. In the early morning hours, all the sleds were used to transport the wounded. The village was under shell fire. We loaded in haste. The operating group, which had remained behind at the main bandaging station, took care of the wounded. The surgeon, Dr. Abderhalden, son of the renowned physiologist, who worked in St. Gallen, Switzerland, after the war, stayed at the operating table to the last minute, then he and his crew directed the loading of the patients onto the sleds that arrived. The enemy had already established itself in another part of the village. The bandaging station was under machine-gun fire. When the last wounded had been taken away to safety, our crew retreated. The surgeon was the last German soldier to leave the place. The German Flak guns, which had taken positions in the valley, took the village under fire and held the enemy back long enough for the operating group and the patients to reach a fairly safe place.

On the next day the village was recaptured. Along with forces of the 4th Panzer Division, we drove the enemy back across the Oka.

The thermometer showed more than thirty degrees below zero in those January days of 1942. Our infantrymen did the incredible in the defense and again in the counterattack. It was reported that enemy cavalry could be expected from the west. Every village had to be built up into a support point. While making holes in the ground, we came upon positions that had been built by the Soviets in October. What a grotesque development that was! We had driven the enemy far back into his own land, thrown him back to the east, and now we were defending ourselves in his old positions and awaiting him from the west.

The main battle line showed a bowlike curve. At night, muzzle flash flared up from all directions, and behind us Flak guns disturbed the quiet of the skies. We began to feel that we were in a pocket and exposed to the ups and downs of the course of fate.

The situation in front of the division's sector was strengthened, and a positional war began. Proper latrines could now be built. We also found time for writing down an experience report: "As opposed to the Russian instructions, the Germans received no information that concerned meeting the needs of the medical service and the care of wounded. The responsibility of making the proper care of the sick and wounded by medical units possible is borne not only by the medical corps in the field but also ultimately by the highest military offices."

Why should the high command not be reminded of such facts? We did not want to give criticism, but felt such a suggestion was necessary. We knew, of course, that the activity in hospitals, at bandaging stations, and all the actions of the medical corps did not at all influence the military operations that were going on. Our work remained more or less inconspicuous and was always the same. In advance, attack, pursuit, defense or retreat—one always saw the same scenes of suffering at our HV stations. The war taught us to endure hard times, and yet we maintained our feeling hearts. In the first weeks of the campaign, we still saw the joy of a gained victory in the faces of the wounded. But in retreat, many miserable pictures of depression, sorrow and anxiety came into view. Just don't leave us behind, they told us with their eyes. The German soldier was brave, including in bearing his pains. They often lay still by the hundreds at our main bandaging stations, much too tired and fought out to complain or groan. Patiently they bore their sorrows, the operations and the changing of bandages. With thankful eyes they looked at the doctor and the medical staff. For us those looks were the reward for our constant service.

When it smelled of powder smoke, blood and ether, and the operating table was shaken by nearby shell hits, when the bullets flew and the iron splinters flew around our noses, the wounded had to be rescued from the minefield and carried over a rise in the enemy's sight and fire—whoever survived here, he too was a brave medical soldier. We had become the infantry's best friends and the wounded men's loyal helpers.

Oberfeldarzt Dr. Hawickhorst

From the Divisions . . .

98th Infantry Division, eastern Campaign, central sector, near Korosten, mid-August 1941:

Both HV stations—that in Jusefovka of the 2nd Medical Company and that in Chepovitzin of the 1st Medical Company—found themselves in exhausting activity. In twelve days the 1st Medical Company received 1253 wounded.

198th Infantry Division, eastern campaign, at the Dniepropetrovsk bridgehead, September 1941:

An advanced surgical group of the 1st Medical Company performed outstandingly at the bridgehead. They had set up their HV station in a cellar, where the numerous wounded could be treated immediately. Although the building above the cellar and the neighboring houses were shattered by enemy shell fire, serious operations and treatment of wounds went on without interruption. The medical skill, the worn and strength of will of the Oberarzt Dr. Runge, can be thanked by many soldiers for their life and health.

98th Infantry Division, eastern campaign, retreat from Moscow to the Istya, December 27, 1941:

A loyal comrade, the regimental doctor of Infantry Regiment 282, Stabsarzt Dr. Schiefelbein, performed exemplary service, was surprised by enemy troops on snowshoes, wounded himself, and fell with the soldiers entrusted to him.

The medical support point in Medyn treated 1640 men in the seven days from November 4 to 11, 1241 of them wounded and 299 sick, mostly of frostbite.

24th Infantry Division, eastern campaign, southern sector, in the winter combat during the first attack on Sevastopol, 1941-42:

The medical and veterinary services of the division came through a hard winter. The high number of wounded in the days of fighting before Sevastopol and the constant treatment of wounded in the difficult positions made the utmost demands on the medical officers and their staffs. Many a quiet act of heroism was performed here. A sergeant of the regimental band of Inf. Reg. 31, for example, spent four months in a makeshift hole in the ground on the steep slope above a rocky gorge. He willingly declined relief and, with his team of two local horses and a small farm wagon, brought the wounded from the bandaging stations near Mekensia to the ambulance park. At the HV stations of the two medical companies in Salonkoy and Cherkes-Kermen, operating, bandaging and other treatment went on day and night; the men were always ready to help.

The field hospital of the division was set up in Baktchissaray.

98th Infantry Division, eastern campaign, retreat from Moscow, early January 1942:

Frequently the transport of wounded from the front was only possible under enemy fire. Corporal Winkler, an ambulance driver, rescued—already wounded himself—five wounded men by spirited driving, disregarding the enemy fire on the southwest slope of Maloyaroslavez. Wounded again as he broke through the enemy fire, he brought the five safely to Medyn.

Scherer Battle Group, eastern campaign, northern sector, Cholm pocket, spring 1942:

The wounded (2200 in all) were operated on by Stabsarzt Dr. Ocker (ranking doctor in the pocket), Oberarzt Dr. Muck and their staff in a low, unprotected space that was hit five times by Russian Pak shells. A wooden sled set on blocks served as an operating table. The surgeons worked in day and night shifts, often only by flickering candlelight. In the 105 days they were surrounded, Assistenzarzt Dr. H. and Unterarzt Dr. G., along with the surgeons, performed 1000 operations and applied 5000 bandages under the most primitive conditions.

56th Infantry Division, eastern campaign, southern sector, spring 1942:

With great dedication, the Division Doctor, Dr. Klein, devoted himself to the completion of medical facilities and setups. Bathing and delousing facilities were set up near the front, and HV stations, which took on a more hospital-like character, made it possible for sick and slightly wounded men could stay with their division until they were healed.

198th Infantry Division, eastern campaign, southern sector, attack on Tuapse, Western Caucasus, summer 1942:

Stabsarzt Dr. Stockdorph and Stabsarzt Dr. Oeding, like all the other doctors, were working tirelessly to treat the wounded in these days. Under the roughest conditions they and their staffs performed their duties.

The Medical Services of the XXXXIX Mtn. A.K. in the Caucasus and at the Kuban, 1942-43

The combat in the Caucasus in 1942 in particular made the highest demands on the medical services on duty there. Along with the fighting troops, they endured not only the enemy action, the bad weather, the shortage of food and the rough terrain in the mountains. They were also faced with almost insoluble problems, which they could surmount only with their most devoted service and the use of every ounce of strength.

After the battles on the endless steppes between the Don and the Caucasus, Jäger and medical corpsmen approached the mountains with a feeling of relief and hope. From the edge of the mountains, the XXXXIX. (Mtn.) Army Corps, with the 1st and 4th Mountain Divisions, had fought its way to the central ridge of the Caucasus in seven days and in ten more days had taken control of eight high mountain passes over 2500 meters above sea level, and even a few over 3000 meters. Until then, the task of the mountain troops and that of the medical troops was fulfillable.

With the Jäger breakthrough over the Kluchor (2816 m) and Adsapch (2579 m) passes and deep down into the Transcaucasian Klitch and Bsyb Valleys, tasks of overwhelming difficulty faced the medical troops, who had never in the history of the war faced such conditions.

However much lower the lands were that the troops won as they approached the end of the mountains, the more problems for the transport of patients were caused by the pathways and the differences in elevation. On the one hand, it was necessary to treat the wounded at advanced HV stations and medical support points, sometimes in the combat areas; on the other hand, the situation was ultimately thus that transporting the wounded first had to be done up height differences of 1800 meters before the actual "transport away" to the medical support points or valley medical facilities on the north side of the Caucasus ridge could begin. Through the exhausting work of the medical corpsmen and stretcher bearers, at times with the help of war prisoners and sometimes with beasts of burden or engineers' cableways, it was possible to move hundreds of wounded men through a chain of medical support points over a path that, in terms of distance and altitude differences, corresponded to the path from Garmisch to Schneefernhaus and back but was far beyond it in terms of difficulty, quite apart from the threat of enemy action.

In this transport by the mountain divisions from their Transcaucasian combat positions to the main ridge. there were 139 wounded in one main bandaging station of the 1st

Mountain Division in the Klitch Valley, 89 of whom had to be transported lying flat, and had to be carried along the endless and wretched path over the Kluchor Pass until, after some days, they could reach the valley hospitals of Teberda and Mokoyan-Shachar. In the five weeks of combat in the zone of the Mountain Corps, 848 wounded in all were transported, which indicates that they needed to be moved.

Different, but no less hard and exhausting, were the demands made on the medical corps a few weeks later in the wooded hills of the western Caucasus. Before it had been the unusual differences in altitude; here it was the rain that poured for weeks, the endless mud and the great distances that brought unheard-of burdens. The wounded had to be carried by stretcher bearers for up to 40 kilometers before it was possible to put them on vehicles. Spread over a broad field of action, the bandaging stations and medical support points were able to do their job even halfway satisfactorily, despite their exhausting efforts, only when it was possible to apply additional personnel and equipment. Here transport depended on the help of war prisoners, plus the troops' tracked vehicles and beasts of burden. But finally even these were exhausted. Thus it was right and justified to carry on constant transport of badly wounded men out of the Gunaika Valley by using medical "Storch" aircraft. For this valuable support in an almost hopeless situation, the Luftwaffe deserves respect. The achievements of the divisions' medical services are proved by the fact that in the constant heavy fighting of the mountain corps from September 1942 to the end of that year, 6932 wounded were treated and transported.

Along with this gigantic burden, the medical corpsmen also had another task. The roughest living conditions in the weeks of rainy and muddy weather threatened to exhaust the troops in terms of hunger, dirt and lice. The doctors and medical personnel had to work hard to decrease, as much as possible, at least the most serious health dangers caused by coldness, dampness, exhaustion and insect pests. Actual epidemics among the troops could be prevented completely. An indication of the demands on the medical services is shown by the casualty statistics of the XXXXIX. (Mtn.) Army Corps. From the time it left its winter position on the Mius in the summer of 1942 to the end of the year, it lost 2942 dead and 11,039 wounded. Among them were 124 dead and 315 wounded among the medical personnel, including stretcher bearers. With every 24 dead and 35 wounded in the mountain corps, they lost a member of the medical services. Another indication of the extent of the task is the fact that, in the withdrawal of the mountain corps from the high and wooded Caucasus in the mountain corps' area, there were set up: 8 hospitals, 16 main bandaging stations and 26 medical support points in the high and moderate mountains, and this is not counting the numerous troop bandaging stations.

Dr. med. A. Wallner,
Prof. Dr. May and
Dr Schulze-Jena.

With Mountain Medical Unit 94 in the high Caucasus in 1942

On reaching the Caucasus, the troops first had to be reorganized for duty in the mountains. After the opening of a field hospital in Pssebaiskaya, main bandaging stations, medical support points and operations groups were loaded onto beasts of burden advanced through the mountains until they reached the troop bandaging stations. In the first combat, the tasks of the medical services were still fulfillable. But the farther the fighting moved over the ridge of the mountains and to the south, the greater were the distances and altitude differences for the wounded to be transported back. After they were brought in and assembled at gathering points, they received their first medical care under the most primitive conditions—in the open air, in small tents or stone bunkers—and then they all, without exception, had to be sent back over gradually organized chains of medical support points on foot. Only from the large valleys that ran out of the mountains could ambulances and trucks take them to the field hospital, and at times the most severely wounded could be flown out from improvised airfields in Fieseler "Storch" planes. But this was possible only in good weather, and not at all in winter.

Whoever was wounded up ahead at the passes or in the ravines had to face an unbelievably rough path. There was no other way, no matter what kind of wounds one had; every wounded man had to be brought to the hospital in three, four or five days' marches through the mountains and valleys.

The slightly wounded, and this included all those who somehow could still walk, had to march themselves out of the mountains. Mountain riflemen with arm or chest wounds, head wounds, broken bones, shell splinters in their bodies or various other wounds hobbled back on canes or supported by likewise wounded comrades, spent their nights with dirty and blood-soaked bandages somewhere in the rocky mountains or the deep forests, dragged themselves farther, got lost, went hungry, and many of them died alone at the edge of the path. Others never arrived and remained missing forever.

The more and most badly wounded had to be carried by four men, with another four to relieve them. When there were no longer enough medical corpsmen and stretcher bearers, the riflemen helped, but so as not to make their dwindling fighting power even weaker irresponsibly, they finally used native civilians and Soviet prisoners of war to transport the wounded, always accompanied by two men of the mountain medical companies. With their swaying stretchers, they stumbled over rock and stone, slipping and scrambling up and down the mountains. The carriers often collapsed from exhaustion, and sometimes the patients, on primitive crossings, fell into swirling mountains streams and had to be rescued laboriously, or had to be lowered on cables over glaciers and landslides. Thus they moved from one support point to the next, where the badly wounded men often lay in damp tents in the rain and waited for further transport, or were treated in dark blockhouses without any modern surgical supplies.

What it was like, for example, in the Urushten Valley early that October was described by several mountain soldiers:

There at Point 1410, where the narrow path from the narrow valley turned off to the "Weaver Hut," stood a few tents and tree-branch huts with a Red Cross flag in the thick bushes—the troop bandaging station of the III./Mountain Jäger Regiment 91. Here only one Assistenzarzt, a medical sergeant and a few helpers were working. On a table made out of a few chopped-down tree trunks, without anesthesia, which was not available here, operations were performed. New wounded men were constantly being brought in, carried in tent canvas or carriers cobbled up from branches and twigs.

Gefreite Tossmann of the 2./94, who had stepped on a box mine hidden in the woods in the Alous Valley around noon on October 7, had to have his shattered left foot removed at this bandaging station. On the next morning, carried on a makeshift stretcher, he was carried on the shoulders of four prisoners, and since at the time there was nobody there who could accompany him, he was given two things—a stick to drive the carriers when they got tired, and a pistol for self-defense, with the last bullet for himself. But the badly wounded Gefreite Tossmann did not need them—the four prisoners carried him steadily and patiently, hour after hour, even when he believed he could no longer stand the pain. It was a real march through hell for three whole days—back to the "Weaver Hut," down to "Fritzdorf" and on to the small village of Kirovski. where an ambulance finally took him to the hospital in Pssebaiskaya. There, because of a gas burn he had suffered meanwhile, a new operation was necessary, in which his whole leg had to be removed.

With Field Hospital 162 on the Eastern Front, 1941 to January 1943

At the end of February 1940 I became the chief doctor of the hospital. The division's medical services were to be used according to the war medical directives. The horsedrawn medical company marched between the infantry and artillery. It set up a main bandaging station and a wagon park, but also utilized the troop bandaging station of a battalion as an advanced bandaging station. The motorized medical company could be moved quickly to form a focal point. After setting up the HV station and wagon park, its main job was treating wounds. Searching the battlefield and bringing men to the HV station were often its jobs too. The two ambulance platoons were to take the wounded to the backlines, particularly the badly wounded—for example, skull, chest and abdominal wounds plus broken bones—to the field hospital for operations, and take the slightly wounded past the field hospital to the army's gathering places.

Because of the extensive distances, this scheme could be followed during the advance in Russia only in rare cases. As a result, the field hospital not only received the wounded from its own division, but all the wounded. It not only took on the function of a gathering place for the army's patients, but since the army seldom moved forward, it also handled transport back to the army's patient gathering places and military hospitals. For this job, the hospital's ambulance platoons, with their trucks and, particularly, two buses were available. Most of the wounded were transported by empty columns, often up to 200 kilometers away. Thank God there was always enough straw to be had in the Ukraine, so that these heavy trucks could be stuffed full of straw, for with their light loads the trucks were practically unsprung. In spite of them, transport was painful enough. At the railroad station in Kovel we could load the patients into passenger cars, thus sparing them the overland transport through the muddy area at the former line of demarcation. Only once in two years were we able to transport two wounded men in a Fieseler "Storch" plane.

In the combat zones we immediately made efforts to get economic life back into operation. Farms, dairies, workshops and the like were soon functioning again, and everywhere we immediately set up a civilian hospital in which, when possible, Russian personnel worked, but we also performed operations.

Thus in many areas we were able to live off the land and extend our capacities. We were set up for 200 beds, but often we expanded to 500, with 400 wounded and sick often arriving in one day.

Other than the problem of transporting the wounded, we had the same problem with our equipment. We already had too little tonnage for the intended equipment, and besides that, there was no room in the prescribed containers for the big balls of bandage material, ether bottles and saline blood substitutes, which were susceptible to heat, cold and breakage. Then too, we also didn't want to leave unplanned-for equipment for a laundry and delousing station behind and have to obtain them again. Certainly we had many vehicles via the KStN (Kriegsstärkenachweisung), but even so, our supply of gasoline was no greater. Therefore we were compelled to perform many treatments categorized sufficiently by the term "injection."

Paragraph 19 of the War Medical Directives (Army) allowed the corps to make use of the divisions' medical units under special situations. Dr. Walter, then the Oberarzt, made extensive use of this the field hospitals in this way, so that there was reasonable functioning, either overlapping or replacing. Under him, I also became accustomed to get information from the corps staff about the situation and suggest my actions afterward. Several very successful actions came to pass. But when the army corps changed, this system usually did not work. But I always received my orders then too, and from four different places, the Army Quartermaster and corps doctor, the Ib of the division and the division doctor. So we could choose what suited us and do what we wanted to do, and we always wanted what we were supposed to do. This nice system would never have worked if we had not had the absolute good will of the army doctor, Dr. Haubenreisser. He was known and feared as a strict leader, but somehow he always had a soft spot in his heart for us.

In the War Medical Directives it said that we were to turn in dirty bed linens and pick up new ones at the medical park. That was impossible. To equip our laundry, we packed bathtubs one inside another and transported them on a gun mount. We also took along to captured field kitchens to heat water. The meat was cooked off dead horses, and from the cooked-out fat our staff pharmacist made clear soap. At our place a wounded man never lay on bare straw. The white-sheeted bed is a great healing factor for the wounded, especially when he has been without it for a long time.

The kitchen also had to be expanded. We had only two 200-liter field kitchens. Not only for the surgical patients, but for the sick ones, we had to prepare a diet. We found a steel plate, 1 x 2 meters. Since most of the women in Russia could lay bricks, we could always have a low oven built using this steel plate, on which large or small pots could stand. At times we prepared nine different diets. We had butchers serving as cooks. Our kitchen chief, the later Master Butcher Burkhard of Regensburg, especially deserves to be recognized. Even his goat soup tasted good.

A major action took place in Chabnoye, eastward of Korosten on the south rim of the Pripyet Marshes. Here we were far back and received up to 400 patients a day from several medical units. The surgical procedures required at least a bandage change, in which gas-burn infections were often diagnosed. We also had to arrange transport to Shitomir. The distance was 180 kilometers, and the roads were bad. Transport was usually done by empty columns.

In Chabnoye, dysentery patients first turned up in large numbers. Fortunately it was not, as in the Polish campaign, the life-threatening Shiga dysentery. The increase in dysentery was attributable on the one hand to the poor latrine discipline of the troops, and on the other hand, the infantrymen had lost so much salt in sweat that they could no longer form stomach acids and thus had no more protection against infection.

Here we also found it necessary to delouse entire units. It was done with hot-air boxes, some of which we had taken from the Russians, while we built the rest ourselves. The showers were also improvised. When the divisions had crossed the Dniepr, the stream of wounded dried up. We moved on, crossed the river north of Kiev, near Ostier, and made a big arc on the eastern shore, so that we finally reached Brovarie from the southeast. In the process we made much unpleasant contact with the Russians fleeing from Kiev.

From Brovarie we set up hospitals for the many Russian prisoners of war. Russian medical units were available, as were butcher and bakery companies and large amounts of Russian provisions. To these hospitals we also took the wounded from two regular hospital trains, which had been bombed and were blocking the tracks.

We increased our fleet of vehicles by modifying captured vehicles to meet our needs. Two minor actions in Yagotin and Mirgorod, where we celebrated Christmas, were followed by very rough marches to Kharkov and Byelgograd, in order to be transferred at last to Merefa, 25 km south of Kharkov. Here we stayed from January 31 to June 6, 1942. Ours was the first hospital for the northern Lossavaya sector.

After the Soviets had broken through here as far as Bereka, the situation was that the railroad line originally ran parallel to the front, then cut across it, so that the Russian and German supply trains were sometimes not very far apart.

The wounded came to us with the daily food supply train, which arrived at some time in the night. Since it was still bitterly cold and the radiators of our vehicles were all leaking, so that there was no way to use anti-freeze, the vehicles stood there with dry radiators. The oil was drained out and put on the stove. The batteries were attached to the charger. One Diesel vehicle ran on the stand and, when the supply train was reported, towed the vehicles that were filled with hot water and oil. They brought the wounded the two kilometers from the station to the hospital, where there were operations every night until about 3 or 4 A.M.

So that they did not have to wait so long, it was later possible to fit two trucks with railroad wheels. These were hooked up so that one truck always had its motor at the front, allowing movement in either direction. They were nicknamed the "hanging dogs."

The wounded who could be transported were taken to Kharkov by day and sometimes also picked up singly by the army.

All abdominal injuries were operated on by us, unless they reached us dying. For these operations we had success figures of 40%. That is a large number, which shows, among other things, that the situation of the abdominal damage was more crucial than the time of the operation, depending on whether it was in the large or small intestine. But that could not always be told with certainty from outside.

Our numerous blood transfusions certainly contributed to our success. The donating process was not simple, and it was also difficult to prevent the transmission of malaria, because the transfusion was done directly from the donor to the recipient with the Olecker device. But we had no transfusion problems, since we only gave transfusions once in a while. I saw them later in the army or group area.

When there were many patients, both surgeons operated simultaneously, and there was still a third table in the operating room, at which one of the non-surgeons worked under the supervision of one of the surgeons, since they were often kept at their case for a long time. Beside the admissions office, the bandaging room was also important, where the medical treatment of the less serious wounds was performed. Here Dr. Bottke, an HNO doctor, did his work successfully. He also carried out the selection of the new arrivals.

The chief was not hesitant about assisting the surgeons subordinate to him, but he could always do only things that did not last too long, for there was much organizational work to do.

The high point of our work in Merefa was in May 1942, in the great battle of Kharkov. Although the Russians were quite hot on our trail and we also had orders to march, we did not move. In front of us was an 88 mm Flak unit that fired on everything that came along, big or small. We had many badly wounded men there, whose transport would have meant sure death. We received high praise from the Generalarzt for our endurance.

On our advance into the great Don sector, our last major action, after several small ones, took place in Meshkov.

The division was in a well-built forward-slope position beside the Don. There were many wounded when attacks on our allies had to be dealt with, but also among our own men. Here for the first time there were more illnesses than trauma cases. Typhus, dysentery, jaundice, nephritis, malaria, five-day fever and isolated cases of other diseases caused the "internals" to fill up 200 beds, as opposed to a surgical section of at most 100 beds. Numerous houses had to be extended and fitted with latrines that met hygienic needs. Problems arose with water supply and particularly electric light.

In the wooded estate of Lipyagie, some 30 kilometers south of Meshkov, we set up a recuperation hospital, since our convalescents were sent back to us from Kharkov in any case. We equipped it with several kolkhozes so that there would be "something good to eat" there. But we also strove for good relations with the local civilians.

At the beginning of December 1942, the division was applied against the enemy, which had broken through at a not completely eliminated bridgehead in the Italian sector. Along with the 22nd Panzer Division, they were able to throw the Russians back 30 kilometers. Then everything broke down to our left and right. The field hospital had moved behind the sector of its division and had set up a 300-bed hospital west of Bokovskaya in the Sovkose Itrasnaya Sarya, and it soon filled up with seriously wounded men. To our misfortune, we also received, on direct orders, 200 slightly wounded men, so that the division would not lose them.

A war-weary Panzer lieutenant came to me and reported that, three kilometers behind the hill, there would be enemies with ten tanks, and that there were no forces between them and us. In two days we were able to move most of the badly wounded out. As we were loading the last thirty onto two trucks on the third day, there was a low-flying air attack that destroyed all the doors and windows but did not accomplish much else. But the slightly wounded men went off with the two trucks, so we had to wait for the return of our column in the evening. Then, as the last wounded were being loaded, the tank attack took place. But an antitank gun left behind by the repair-shop company held them off so that the men reached the hospital safely.

In the days that followed, we lost many vehicles and much equipment, because we had to make two trips, and we always met the Soviets on the second trip. On the day before Christmas Eve, we passed through Morosovskaya and reached the village of Tchekalov, south of it, without being in touch with the division.

On Christmas Day we were able to make contact with the division again, and we opened a hospital in Morosovskaya that evening. There we worked until December 31, then we moved with the division across the Donets on the ice bridge at Balki and back to Krasny Sulin in the vicinity of Chakty. On February 5 the news reached me there that I had been commanded to hygienic training as of the past December 18.

In the time that followed, the hospital was involved in a few minor actions, and was then taken over by the division and army field hospital. In those days there were many changes of chief doctors, and by the end of the war it had moved back to Salzburg.

Oberstabsarzt Dr. Baumeister (ret.)

A stroke of luck—only a flesh wound.

Troop Illness Report (not including wounded) of the 1st Mountain Division, December 1-10, 1942.

1. The nutrition and strength condition of the combat units serving in the front lines is all the worse because their practical loss everywhere has to be reckoned with. Through the unbroken rainy weather of the last four weeks and the resulting supply difficulties involving food and warm clothing, as well as being housed in thoroughly soaked bunkers and holey tents, an extraordinary increase in susceptibility to disease has developed. The men are completely emaciated and so weakened by the strains of combat with insufficient nutrition that physical achievement in mountain warfare can no longer be attained.

2. The new cases of epidemic jaundice have decreased, but on the other hand, stomach and intestinal catarrh, bladder infections, kidney diseases and general colds (bronchial catarrh, etc.) have been increasing steadily. Since the reduced fighting strength of the front line cannot be allowed to decrease further, most of these sick men have been kept in their positions.

3. For weeks there has been no way to provide bodily care for the troops at the front. What with the general filth in their wet clothing, skin diseases of all kinds have appeared.

4. The first cases of first and second degree frostbite have occurred in the time covered by this report.

5. There is still a high degree of infestation by lice.

6. The water that is, to be sure, so plentiful in the valley is so dirty and muddy that it cannot be used as it is for cooking. In the mountains, water is taken from branches or small brooks, but its condition cannot be presupposed to be potable, what with the dead bodies, frequently found in the woods but often very hard to remove, and visible animal cadavers.

7. The majority of the entire division, including the supply services, bivouacs in tents, bunkers and dugouts.

8. Food for the troops is on hand in sufficient quantities. The units in the front lines, though, receive their food only irregularly on account of the tremendous supply difficulties, since on the supply paths, partly because of enemy action, partly because of the weather or high water at the fords, portions of the food are lost again and again.

9. Clothing is also on hand in sufficient quantities. But it is not possible to move the received clothing (winter coats, chest and back warmers, head protectors, gloves and footwear) forward. Thus the clothing of the men in the front lines is catastrophically bad. It is not only fully insufficient against weather and coldness, but also constantly soaked through, dirty, torn and worn out.

10. No other particular observations.

Division Doctor Dr. Kittler

The number of wounded and sick sent out from September 27 to December 31, 1942 numbered 6214 men, including 196 officers. The marching time for the carriers from the foremost positions to the Guinaika Valley to meet horsedrawn and motorized vehicles (tracked motorcycles) amounts to three days.

The Medical Services of the 1st Mountain Division in Russia in the Spring of 1943

Division Doctor, Div.St.Qu., April 30, 1943
1st Mountain Division
Az. 49 s
Re: Activity Report
To 1st Mountain Division/Ib

The Activity Report is divided into the time periods from Jan. 1 to Jan. 24, 1943—combat in the western Caucasus, southeast of the Maikop-Tuapse road—Withdrawal movements of the remaining parts of the division in the central Caucasus, Jan. 25-April 8, 1943, withdrawal movements of the entire division from the Caucasus area, through the Kuban area as far as Kertch. Rail transport from there to Serbia.

Combat in the western Caucasus.

The prepared means of the medical services for the period from January 1 to April 24, 1943 were already made in the previous months. The medical services to the division were assured by the mountain HV station and support points in the valley, from which the wounded were transported by ambulance to Apcheronskaya and Neftyanaya.

For the transport of wounded, there were available: 60 Russian prisoners of war apiece for Mountain Medical Co. 1/54 and the two V companies = in all 120 bearers; transport by ambulance was conducted by the two ambulance companies 1/54 and 2/54.

The medical care was provided by Mountain Medical Co. 1/54, Mountain Medical Co. 1/901 and 2/901 (V), and Field Hospital 54.

Taking part were:

Mountain Medical Co. 1/54 with one valley HV station in Neftyanaya and two medical support points.

Mountain Medical Co. 1 and 2/901 with the mountain HV station on Mount Lyssa and one medical support point.

Field Hospital 54 as HV station and field hospital in Apcheronskaya, Ambulance Platoon 1/54 with vehicle stopping places in Susdalski and Navaginski Hf.

The troops were housed in wooden bunkers at forest positions. As long as there was no dew, the housing was relatively good. A part of the troops bivouacked in tents. The weather, cold and dry until the middle of the report period, turned to wet weather. Immediately the cases of frostbite increased, especially of feet. There were no epidemics, other than increased numbers of sick with diarrhea. The shortenings of the front, carried out as planned, improved the supply situation markedly, so that medical materials were available to the troops in sufficient quantities.

Withdrawal movements out of the Caucasus area:

Bearer columns. consisting of Russian prisoners of war, were detailed to the marching groups by the Division Doctor. Actions were determined by the Regimental Doctor. At the same time, every marching group was assigned a main bandaging station. These actions were likewise determined by the Regimental Doctor.

The division got out of the Caucasus without notable personnel losses and, north of the Kuban, entered the area of Usti-Labinskaya, Dinskaya and Plastunovskaya, joining the parts of the division that came from the central Caucasus. The medical services of these units (Mountain Jäger Regiment 99) was provided until then by Mountain Medical Co. 2/54. The division doctor had succeeded in loading up all the medical equipment and supplies and bring it to the area north of the Kuban, mainly by rail. After the division arrived there, search actions were undertaken to locate the loaded materials, but only some of the equipment was found. The majority of the cars loaded with the medical materials must have been blown up when the enemy drew near.

The troops had the opportunity to supply themselves liberally with winter clothing at abandoned depots while on the march from the Maikop area to the area north of the Kuban.

The troops also took advantage of the opportunity to supply themselves with valuable provisions. Thanks to this, their health improved markedly, despite all their marches.

North of the Kuban the medical situation was as follows: Field Hospital 54 was sent on the march into the backline area in the direction of Temryuk after the division doctor arrived. It arrived there without personnel or material losses.

Mountain Medical Co. 1/54 was fully ready for action, with two main bandaging stations.

Mountain Medical Co. 2/54, coming from the central Caucasus, had to destroy 50% of its vehicles and could set up only one motorized HV station. Mountain Medical Co. 1 and 2/901 (V) were minus all equipment and weakened just as much in personnel. What remained of both companies was gathered for one HV station. It was made ready for action with makeshift equipment.

Thus there were three horsedrawn HV stations available. Moving the sick and wounded was done by Ambulance Platoons 1/54 and 2/54, combined into one company. Until the mud season began, there were no particular difficulties in the medical services. Delivery of medical materials from the backline areas did not take place. But their needs could be met fully with supplies left behind along the way by other divisions.

Shortly before the mud season began, the HV Station (mot.) 2/54 was sent marching as far back as possible to set up a hospital at Slaviyanskaya, Even after the mud season began, it was possible to transport the sick and wounded to Ivanovskaya by the ambulance company. The mud season, which set in here in all its muddiness, eliminated the ambulance as a means of transport. It was possible to tow some of the ambulances to Slaviyanskaya with the help of towing tractors. Ambulances that were not able to make it had to be destroyed. The transport of wounded was done from then on by horsedrawn vehicles (empty columns of the division's supply train).

On the march out of Ivanovskaya, the HV station had to abandon and destroy all its equipment because of unconquerable mud, just to be able to move the wounded men. A farm wagon had to be pulled by eight horses to get through, and only two patients could be carried on a wagon.

In Slaviyanskaya the bandaging station was again equipped in a makeshift manner. The necessary equipment could be taken out of abandoned railroad trains. To make it mobile, the division, on request of the division doctor, made eight four-horse Hf. 3 available.

Mountain Medical Co. 1/54 took over the local hospital in Slaviyanskaya from Mountain Medical Co. 2/54. As the weather improved, the motorized HV Station 2/54 could set out for Anastasievskaya and set up an HV station there. From Slaviyanskaya, the sick and wounded were sent by air, and sometimes by ship, to the Kuban.

w medical supplies arrived by air as well, so that there was never any lack of medical materials.

In Slaviyanskaya the first cases of typhus in the division were noted. The division was completely overrun with lice. The constant marches left no time to carry out the strict measures required against typhus. According to the troop doctors' observations, typhus was brought in mainly from ex-prisoners who had been in inconceivably wretched physical conditions. It must be stressed that the division, despite the difficulties of the withdrawal, still found the time for physical hygiene. Individual units set up makeshift delousing stations quickly and thus could stop the spread of lice. The remarkably limited living conditions, though, soon wiped out all the success that had been gained.

In Anastasievkaya the mud season came to an end. The few ambulances still available could again be used to transport the wounded. The motorized HV Station 2/54 was sent on the march to Kerch.

When they left Anastasievkaya, the division was sent to march in the direction of Kerch. The medical service was then provided by Kr.S.P. Every marching group was also assigned one ambulance.

Field Hospital 54 had already been transferred to Kerch and settled down in the Seitler area.

After the transfer over the narrows at Kerch, the individual units were immediately loaded onto the train. The delousing facilities available in Kerch were not sufficient to serve the crowds of arriving soldiers. Thus it was that the great majority of the division remained undeloused.

During their rail transport, there were a few cases of typhus, which were disembarked along the way. It was impossible to delouse the whole division during transport. Just a few groups were deloused in Bucharest.

Personnel losses in the report period of 1/1/43 to 4/10/43

	\multicolumn{3}{c}{Dead}	\multicolumn{3}{c}{Wounded}	\multicolumn{3}{c}{Missing}	\multicolumn{3}{c}{Sick}
	O.	B.	U. & M.	O.	B.	U. & M.	O.	B.	U. & M.	O.	B.	U. & M.
1/1-1/10/43	-	-	3	1	-	31	-	-	-	7	1	247
1/11-1/20/43	-	-	14	2	-	39	-	-	-	4	-	190
1/21-1/31/43	2	-	34	1	-	90	-	-	10	6	-	391
2/1-2/10/43	1	-	13	-	-	61	-	-	18	2	-	238
2/11-2/20/43	-	-	51	2	-	97	-	-	21	3	-	146
2/21-2/28/43	-	-	15	2	1	43	-	-	12	3	-	109
3/1-3/10/43	-	-	47	5	-	186	-	-	3	4	-	141
3/11-3/20/43	-	-	16	3	-	55	-	-	2	3	-	183
3/21-3/31-43	-	-	7	1	-	37	-	-	-	2	-	199
4/1-4/10/43	-	-	-	-	-	2	-	-	-	2	1	113
Total	3	-	200	17	1	641	-	-	66	36	2	195

At a Bandaging Station of the SS Panzer Division "Das Reich" in Russia

Day and night there was no rest at the HV station in Veretenki. Since the wounded were infested with lice, we got lice too. There were many seriously wounded men, numerous amputations, abdominal and lung wounds, broken bones. And with it, we had the sad certainty that all of them, who urgent needed rest, had to be transported out in a short time, which was not good for them under these conditions. And the uncertainty of knowing that there was not enough transport available at the right time got on our nerves.

There were wonderful, clear, frostless nights and enchanting scenes in the snow-covered woods. But did anybody look at that?

In the few minutes one could spare from one's bloody work, from the operating and bandaging rooms, one went to the houses in which the patients lay, to examine them, bandage them, and seek out those ready for transportation. Meanwhile came the report that new wounded, eight or twenty, had once again arrived.

In the operating room, one quickly ate a bit of bread and took a sip of coffee, because a pause had to be made now to get rid of the bloody bandages, the cut-off scraps of skin, the bloody swabs, scraps of uniforms and amputated limbs. There was a pause for that long, until new wounded were brought in again.

One's eyes began to shut, one slept standing up, tears threatened to fall out of one's eyes, one's legs were without feeling, one got sick of the bloody work, the lice bit, and when the next wounded man lay on the table, one just naturally concentrated on him, as if he were the first, and as if one were fully rested. The air was thick enough to cut from the necessary heat, and because the instrument sterilizer was constantly running. And because of the many men who worked here close together, the many smells and exhalations—and all that in a Russian house, where it already smelled of cabbage, stale bread and musty clothing.

Because of the winter cold, the wounded could not be undressed and prepared for treatment in another room first. The wounds were freed for bandaging by cutting the uniform away, and then they were bandaged. Often it was found that, in addition to the one wound, there were others, or that only the entry wound was bandaged. Since the stream of wounded kept flowing constantly, on account of the evacuation of Istra, and we were the bandaging station nearest to the front, we sometimes felt as if we were going crazy....

From the War Diary of a Medical Unit in Russia in 1943

1/1/1943: Number of wounded ca. 800, bedridden 300. Housed in the local hospital and earth bunkers, some in troop billets, in cellars, cellarways: 400. The rest in stone houses, on first and second floors. Because of necessarily rushed removal resulting from failure of transport means, 290 wounded left behind. Here again, heavy losses of medical equipment, materials and provisions. Straw and woolen blankets insufficient. Number of personnel ready for action in Med. Co.: 4 medical officers, 1 official, 32 NCO and man. Unterarzt Steigmüller died of wounds. Oberarzt Sattler missing. Vacancies filled by medical personnel of the troops and slightly wounded men. Condition of exhaustion very serious. Troops hit hard, nourishment insufficient. Contagious diseases, diarrhea without significance. No typhus, sufficient water.

1/9/1943: HV station in local barracks given up, occupied by enemy. Materials rescued. Setting up new HV station not possible for lack of housing. Operating group in eastern part. Wounded were housed in troop housing Jan. 9. Bandaging material still sufficient at time thanks to delivery. Several cases of very mild diphtheria, gas edema, lack of serum. Losses among badly wounded under fire. Number of wounded cannot be given at this time, since no overview is possible because of continued transportation.

1/10/1943: Russian hospital fired on and burned out, some 20 in Russian hands. Wounded have makeshift beds in cellars and stables. Provisions, water holes exhausted. Growing losses under fire. Regulated overview no longer possible.

Wounded situation becomes more catastrophic by the hour. Improvement scarcely to be expected for lack of everything. Diarrhea increasing strongly for last two days. Troops very hindered by housing wounded with them.

1/11/1943: Unterarzt Kaufmann missing. Assistenzarzt Eggert wounded, otherwise all doctors are well.

1/12/1943: Situation of wounded no longer describable or manageable. Operation groups no longer able to work. Doctors divided among areas. Wounded men wandering around all over, further losses among them.

Other Divisions Reported...

78th Infantry Division, eastern campaign, central sector, 1943:

There was a battalion doctor who—badly wounded himself, continued to do his duty as the troop bandaging station of his battalion for several hours, until the last wounded man was treated. Only then did he let himself be taken to the HV station.

11th Infantry Division, eastern campaign, northern sector, summer combat on the Volkov, 1943:

Here too, all the doctors and medical corpsmen served to the end, many had lost their lives, including Dr. von Wiek and Dr. Krause. After their loss, Oberarzt Dr. Nolte, with his staff, had cared for a sector all alone. Stabsarzt Dr. Beck and his helpers handled the HV station in Kelkovo.

56th Infantry Division, eastern campaign, central sector, defensive combat around Orel in June 1943:

The loss statistics offer clear evidence of the hardness of the fighting and the focal-point participation of the division in the very first days of the battle. From the beginning of the battle on July 11 to July 15, 1229 wounded men were treated by the division's two HV stations. Here the self-sacrificing activity of our medical services deserves special honor. In the fateful month of July, their losses numbered six medical officers wounded, 15 medical NCOs dead, 57 wounded and 12 missing.

198th Infantry Division, eastern campaign, southern sector, battle near Byelgogrod, summer 1943:

In addition, Assistenzarzt Dr. Rüdiger stood out because of his selfless treatment of the wounded, despite the heaviest machine-gun and rifle fire; he was one of the last to leave his position, and then was shot in the chest and wounded while withdrawing.

24th Infantry Division, eastern front, northern sector, retreat fighting in the Luga bridgehead, winter 1943-44:

On January 31, 1944 a firefight at close range developed, in which two company chiefs, the battalion doctor and many engineers of Engineer Battalion 24 were lost. Meanwhile, the enemy was attacking from the east in fast advances against the rear guard, so that the few vehicles had to be blown up so as not to let them fall into enemy hands. The survivors of Engineer Battalion 24 joined in. The slightly wounded were taken along. The Division Doctor took care of the badly wounded by hitching horses, with the help of the mounted platoon, to 32 farm wagons. There he was surprised by the Soviets, and the rescue work no longer succeeded. The unit doctor of the intelligence unit and several medical corpsmen fell into enemy hands; the Division Doctor set out alone through the woods and reported back on January 2.

198th Infantry Division, western front, 1944, breakthrough north of Montelimar on August 29, 1944:

Among the many killed that day was the Division Doctor, who treated the wounded, ignoring the heaviest American artillery fire, until a splinter hit him fatally.

Report of the 101st Jäger Division on their Medical Services, 1943-44

Structure: The 1st and 2nd Platoons of the 1st (Mtn.) Medical Co. 101 were stretcher-bearer platoons. They were, as needed, used with the Jäger regiments, the HV station or the motor park. Their job was transporting the wounded to the HV (main bandaging) station.

The 3rd Platoon operated the main bandaging station. Along with the operating and care groups, it included: the "stall" with the beasts of burden and the farm wagons, the field kitchen, the writing room, the dental station, the field pharmacy and the handworkers.

In the 4th Platoon were all the ambulances and trucks, with the repair shop troop.

During the 13 months of service of the 1st (Mtn.) Medical Co. 101 in the Caucasus and the Kuban bridgehead, 15,496 patients passed through the various HV stations, an estimated 3000 of them being sick.

The company's own losses in this period numbered 62 men, 12 dead, 43 wounded and 8 missing.

Of the medical services of the 101st Jäger Division in the period from 3/12 to 4/10/1944 (pocket and breakthrough of the 1st Panzer Army), the following wounded and sick were treated and transported out:

1st Medical Co. 101: 3450
2nd Medical Co. 101: 1415
Field Hospital 101: 9325

Near Lemberg in the summer of 1944:

July 27: The news of the almost complete annihilation of the 2nd Platoon arrives. Jäger Regiment 229, in the Vinniki area, was surrounded and had the task of fighting its way to the southwest. While the spearheads with the foremost parts broke through the enemy barrage line, the Russian counterattack struck the following heavy weapons and supply trains, as well as the men of the 2nd Platoon under the command of Assistenzarzt Dr. Pflieger. The Russians shot Dr. Pflieger when he tried to surrender with the wounded men, who were beaten to death on the farm wag-

57

ons. Only a few of the men were able to escape at first. The sad news of the day: Dr. Pflieger and one man dead, two men wounded, fifteen missing.

The HV station at Turka (in the Carpathians), at which 783 men had been treated since August 10, 1944, had to be evacuated on September 25.

A serious crisis developed, for there were still close to 300 wounded lying in the town. All the vehicles capable of being used were underway somewhere on the pass road, which was occupied by columns of several divisions.

But Turka had a railroad station, and the rails did not seem to be sabotaged. Thus the company chief, Dr. Schückle, set out with Medical Obergefreite Rötter on the way to the backline area in the vague hope of finding a locomotive somewhere. One was indeed found, but without a crew. The railroad men had long since hit the road.

Rötter was able, with the help of a Slovak civilian, to get the locomotive going and hook on several cars. Rötter, who had never before stood on the footplate of a locomotive, now drove it at full speed up the hill to Turka. When he reached the station there, he was so overjoyed that he blew the whistle several times.

But the shrill whistle alarmed the Russian artillery. As if by a miracle, nobody was wounded despite the heavy fire. After 300 wounded had been loaded, the Turka HV station was abandoned at 5:00 PM.

The 1st (Mtn.) Medical Co. 101 had covered 5737 kilometers in Russia. Along with this much marching, the company had transported 39,936 wounded and sick from the troop bandaging stations to the HV stations, mostly under the roughest conditions, treated them optimally there, and send them on to back-line medical facilities.

67 members of the company were killed or missing, 162 were wounded (as far as can be determined).

A medical company is loaded for rail transport.

Doctors and Patients Report

A Troop Doctor before Narvik in May 1940

Our position ran in a semicircle around Ankenes, which stretches over the high plateau of Ankenesfjell, and was held by a company. The climb up to it took a good walker two to three hours and led through pathless thick woods full of underbrush, across brooks and ditches, and later over rocky terrain. To transport the wounded out we often required up to eight hours until we arrived back in Ankenes, covered with sweat. Every time I had to take part in the transport myself, since I had only three men and the transport could only be carried out by four men. It made the greatest demands on the stretcher bearers, as on the patient. Every few steps, one of the stretcher bearers plunged into steep rocky country or into the watercourses of the melting snow and pulled the stretcher with him. In the steep, thick woods it was often maddening when one could not carry the heavy stretcher between the underbrush and the tree trunks. To make things worse, there were always clearings and gun positions to pass, at which machine-gun barrels or the threat of ships' guns aimed at the land made us hurry all the more. In the last days, the marching route constantly led us under enemy artillery fire. Often we lay coughing behind a boulder when this damned "blessing" crashed down a few meters from us. During our first service on the front line, we often got into close combat, in which hand grenades flew back and forth over us. When we then left our cover with the stretcher, the bullets whistled around our ears, so that we ran, stumbled, coughed, set down the stretcher behind cover, and ran again right after that. In every case I immediately gave the patient a morphine ampule on the spot, but it usually proved during the risky transport that a second ampule was needed. When an attack was going on all along the five-kilometer front line in the mountains, then as soon as we had exhausted ourselves moving a wounded man out of a flank position, we had to climb back up again to fetch another patient from the other wing, or from another position. In such cases there was neither day nor night for us; once we were underway constantly for 36 hours. In addition, the wounded at the troop bandaging station naturally had to be treated and cared for regularly. Again and again there were frostbite cases, for the fighting troops in the higher positions had no place to live; they made scouting trips by night and slept by day, as long as the combat events allowed. We never had any replacement or reserve troops. On May 27 a company of Mountain Jäger Regiment 137, who had been parachuted into Björnfjell a few days before, reached us in Ankenes. The day was relatively quiet. But our instincts, trained by combat, made this sudden cessation of military activity seem positively uncanny to us. It was a "calm before the storm" mood. Toward midnight, the "dance" began with a vigor we had never before experienced. Warships were out in the fjord, firing all their guns. In a few minutes, numerous houses were in flames before our eyes, and over in Narvik we saw flames and smoke too. At first the enemy systematically kept our ground positions under fire, and then the droning shells were directed at the village and the slopes. Splinters whistled around our hospital, hit the water hissing, the ground shook, the air was full of smoke and flashes of light. And then grenade-launcher fire increased, along with the rattling of machine guns and the barking of infantry weapons that added to the mad dance. The fighting up above was in full swing! Amid the hail of thousands of bullets, my medical corporal, who was on duty at the company command post, came running back. He was bleeding heavily and quite exhausted. An examination showed that his shoulder blade was smashed. He reported that there were wounded men up ahead. I set out with my other medics. We went springing from house to house in the constant booming and banging. Several times a shell fell very close to us, shell fragments flew over us, windows rattled, earth was thrown up before our eyes. One never knew in which direction to seek shelter, for the enemy was looking directly at our backs from his mountain positions.

For a short time during the action, we lay among the men of a mountain parachute troop. The group was spotted, machine-gun bursts hissed between us, dug up the ground, whistled through the leaves and twigs of the trees; one man was wounded. Then we got back to the troop bandaging station. Several slightly and moderately wounded men had dragged themselves there. I tried to treat them as best I could, made bandages and put in stitches, using my instruments in alcohol, and gave morphine injections to ease the pain. My station filled more and more. Riflemen dragged badly wounded comrades to me, I worked feverishly. Reports came from the right wing, to which the climb normally took three hours, but in today's situation, because of working our way through the heaviest enemy fire, it would take much longer. I could not be away from my patients that long. I had to stay there and be there for all who were brought to me bloody and weak. This insane tumult had already lasted for seven hours, the infantry fire up above slacked off, became slower. More and more exhausted and bleeding soldiers with torn uniforms came down from the heights and crouched apathetically in the ditches outside. Up there all was lost, it was impossible to hold off such superior power, some of them said. It was reported to me that on the left wing there were two badly wounded men, one man with an abdominal wound. Then a lieutenant who had commanded that position was brought down with a knee-joint wound. He told me that the position has been pushed back, the badly wounded could no longer be rescued. I also had an impossible time, with sixteen badly wounded men lying in the rooms of my bandaging station already. If only this house is not hit, was my constant prayer. The thought of the two wounded men who lay bleeding alone in that abandoned position and would probably have to die far from their comrades was a terrible burden on my soul. Enemy soldiers with severe wounds were brought in; they were treated just like our soldiers and movingly expressed their thanks.

Stabsarzt Dr. Puschnig

For Him the War was Over in 1940

A messenger of Mountain Jäger Regiment 100 reported on his severe wound in the evening attack on the bridge over the Aisne-Oisne Canal in the French campaign on June 5, 1940:

We called the command to our platoons. I shook hands with my friend from the next platoon, we wished each other lots of luck, and then the race through the French artillery fire began. The shots boomed everywhere, the big guns thundered with deafening noise, dug up the earth, flattened the fields, tore up trees and bushes. Everybody rushed to where a shallow hollow or a damp ditch offered the slightest cover, to feel safe for a few moments. Nothing helped; again the mad rush forward began. Merciless and horrible, death struck with glowing shards of iron and sharp-edges splinters, sometimes striking home, sometimes grazing us and sometimes coming awfully close...

Then one pressed himself against the ground, happy to have had a little luck, and waited for the next shot. Fountains of earth rose up, dust, smoke and dirt filled the air, and out of this cloud, attacking men always stood up and pushed forward, raced through the iron hail of bursting shells. One no longer thought, no longer hoped, one just rushed from cover to cover. Comrades lay shattered on the ground, with serious wounds they waited for help, and the medics ran here and there, knelt beside the wounded and tried to apply first aid, sometimes in vain.

I had good cover just then and wanted to use the slight pause to catch my breath for the next rush, held my rifle in my right hand and wanted to hold myself on the ground with my left; then suddenly I sensed a burning pain on my left elbow, so a saucer-size shell fragment, felt a twitching in my fingertips and immediately grabbed for my left hand. But I grabbed emptiness; the hand hung down, it didn't belong to me any more. All this happened in seconds, and at the first moment when I noticed the scrap of hot iron, I knew that my hand was lost. The blood flowed over my dusty, dirty uniform; it was over for me. A medic was on the scene at once, bound up my upper arm and put on a temporary bandage. The enemy guns fired on and on, the earth shook when the shells landed, and my comrades kept on advancing. We called a few parting words and good wishes to each other; they had soon gotten through the barrage-fire zone, and I was left alone. Dead and wounded like myself lay all around. Young men who had looked forward to life so much and would so gladly have returned home. I did not want to give up. Though I had lost my left hand, my clear mind, my eyes, my legs and my right hand remained mine. And I knew that I should get home again.

For half an hour I sat there and watched the shells land. I had taken the strap of my steel helmet between my teeth and bitten it on account of the pain. The cold coffee in my field flask, that was supposed to last the whole day, quenched my nagging thirst. Only now did I see that my binoculars were broken in the middle. A strange feeling overcame me. If I had not worn the glasses, then the splinter would have pierced my chest, then it would be all over. Then it occurred to me that I had never had binoculars; only last night had I asked a wounded Jäger for a pair. So it happened that the devilish shell fragment had not been able to do me more harm.

The strap of my steel helmet was bitten through, the field flask was empty, the company was gone from my field of vision. I still could not believe that my career as a soldier was now ended. Now another member of the company would be the messenger to the First Platoon, and when the casualty list was made up tonight, I too would be on it. Yesterday I had written that list.

Waiting until I was fetched seemed too long and too dangerous to me, and so I went back to the troop bandaging station. On the way I met our regimental commander with a rifle in his hand; he asked me about the company's situation and gave me a drink from his field flask.

It had become quiet, and the late evening sank down gently on the torn-up land. In the cellar of a house, in front of which a Red Cross flag hung, I was given an injection, the pains diminished and was half asleep. Wounded men were carried in, some of them acquaintances. We nodded to each other and asked about friends in other companies. Then I was driven to the main bandaging station and on to the field hospital. The medics helped however they could. One of them cut my uniform shirt to free my arm and shattered hand. The wound looked terrible, the fingers were already cold and yellow. My name was called, I was carried into the operating room and laid on the table. A well-known professor was the regimental chief doctor in the division's field hospital. He tried to tell me what to expect. But I already knew, I had been aware the whole day that when I next woke up I would not have my left hand any more. I counted slowly and strongly to 28, but at 29 I went to sleep..."

On the Front Line as a Regimental Doctor

We still lay in our dugouts. Then an artilleryman ran up to us and shouted, still from some distance: "Medics! Doctor!" At the advance post of the mounted artillery unit, which had been set up in the vicinity of their observation post, the artillery officer had been wounded. My Oberfeldwebel and I crawled out of our dugout, reported to the commander and followed the soldier.

We soon saw the position of the artillery observer and ran crouching up the hill. From up there they waved to us; we should crawl up to them. I cam up the hill from behind, without seeing the enemy, found that the officer, a corpulent major, had an abdominal wound, and prepared the injections. I could not straighten up; everything had to be done lying or crouching down. When the Oberfeldwebel had likewise crawled up the hill, we put a tent canvas under the heavy body and set out to slide the major down the hill on the sand and grass.

Once we could stand up straight, we tried to carry the heavy man in the tent canvas. The major had wanted to inspect the enemy position closely with his telescope, had straightened up too much, and had then been hit by a shell fragment. It had wounded two others only slightly. For the time being they could stay under cover and later, as the firing decreased, be treated by their own troop doctor.

All Medical Skill Was In Vain

It was on a hot, sunny July day in Pechinegi on the Donetz in the Ukraine. Our medical company had set up an advanced bandaging station in a school building, so as to be able to treat, as quickly as possible, the wounded we expected from the assault on the strongly fortified Russian positions. The enemy had dug in deeply over the winter, in order to halt our further advance, and one had to expect a bitter defense. Therefore our side employed heavy artillery, and from a nearby airfield there came one string of bombers after another, flying over our heads to unload their deadly freight some two kilometers from us. The ceaseless thunder of the guns blended with the heavy explosions of the bombs.

Scarcely had this dreadful inferno of the war been going on for half an hour when the first wounded were brought to us. I was serving as the surgical assistant to Dr. Fellner's operation group, since there were no patients to treat in my dental station on such a day. Other than a few slightly wounded men, some badly wounded comrades had arrived already. One soldier, about 18 or 19 years old, was in deep shock and had to be treated at once. After he had been undressed, the nature and location of his wound were determined on the operating table, so that the proper surgical treatment could begin. A shell fragment had entered his abdominal cavity from the front and had torn open an exit wound some 5 x 5 centimeters on the side of his back, over the hip. When the surgeon looked more closely at the wound, he found oatmeal mixed with lentils, which had poured out of his damaged intestine. Without a word, Dr. Fellner pointed to what he had found, a gesture that expressed the hopelessness of any surgical skill, and that nothing else could be done. The wounded man was very weak, but fully conscious. He must have seen on our faces that he was very badly wounded, since he asked our surgeon if he had to die. "Please tell me, Herr Oberarzt," were his words, "must I die? I don't want to complain, if I must die, there are so many who must die—but then I have one big request: give me a whole lot to drink, I have a terrible thirst! But if I should have the slightest chance of surviving, then I'll gladly endure the thirst, even if it lasts for weeks." All of us who stood around the operating table turned our eyes to our experienced and warm-hearted Dr. Fellner to see how he would answer. Would he destroy the soldier's last hopes with the horrible truth or pretend to this brave young man with a goodhearted lie? Without thinking for long, the surgeon made reply: "How it turns out depends in part on you—for no liquid must get into your damaged intestine—when you awaken from the ether, then you can take a teaspoon of water in your mouth every five minutes, but you must not swallow it!" "I'll promise you that gladly," was the answer, and with a hopeful "Thank you," the young fellow let him put on the ether mask so that the necessary operation could be performed.

Although the sorrow, the pain and the many deaths in our main bandaging station had hardened us in many ways, yet we were hit very hard when we learned, a few hours later, that death had snuffed out this young life too.

From the Diary of a Doctor

In the diary notes of Stabsarzt Dr. Pappenberger of the 2nd (mot.) Mountain Medical Unit 54 in 1941, the first year of the eastern campaign, he states, among other things:

"Oct. 2: I am asked by a Russian farmer to help his wife. It was a premature birth. Painkillers will bring comfort.

Belosyerka, on the southeast edge of town, the HV station was set up in a roomy schoolhouse. At 6:00 PM we are ready for service. Slowly it gets warm in the rooms, and now the first wounded arrive.

There were terrible wounds among them, noteworthy numbers of abdominal wounds. The poor fellows lay on the battlefield more than 24 hours and could not be rescued earlier on account of the very strong enemy fire. They all had to die. The nature of the various wounds was so terrible that I neither can nor want to list them separately. In any case, we spent the whole night in the operating room. After 7:00 AM the worst of the work was already finished. After a short sleep until 11:00, I worked alone the whole afternoon. Wounded and septic cases alternated.

In the course of the day, a Russian air force lieutenant who had been shot down by a German fighter was brought in. His plane crashed in flames some six kilometers from here. He himself tried to parachute out, but as his chute opened only a short distance above the ground, it only slowed his falling speed a little bit. He was a tall, ruggedly built fellow. Among his papers was the picture of his very pretty fiancee. In examining him, I found that he had a bad skull fracture with compression, serious damage to his lower spinal column with transverse paralysis, and a supramalleolar fracture of the lower thighbone. With such massive injuries, there was nothing more to be done. He was very restless, had great pain and was given much morphine, and SEE three hours later. He died an hour after that and was buried next to our dead.

On the next day, October 3, we had a lot of work changing bandages, cleaning wounds, etc. Newly wounded men also arrived. We had the whole place full and could not take any more in the three prepared houses. There was a lot to do. Our wounded were in generally good condition, but several amputees and men with abdominal wounds died.

Nov. 4: Today our wounded and sick are being transported out. The drivers of the ambulances and their aides are under a lot of pressure. Meanwhile, operations and wound treatment continue. . . .

Thus the Author Received his First Wound at the Kuban Bridgehead in 1943

On the afternoon of May 7 we beat back a massed Soviet attack. While most of the enemies fled back into the woods, numerous dead and wounded lay in the open field. As I, company leader of the 2nd Co., Mtn. Jäger Battalion 94, examined the loopholes of my men, in order to look to the right, I suddenly felt a heavy blow to my upper left thigh, that threw me down. "I'm hit," I realized, and as I opened my mountain trousers, I saw how my shirt and underpants kept turning redder. A messenger who accompanied me knelt next to me, and while I pushed my trousers far down, he opened a package of bandages with his dirty fingers. That was an infantry bullet—it must have come from one of the wounded

Russians lying in the field. It was about 4:00 PM. Carefully we crawled back under cover, I called a Feldwebel to turn the company leadership over to him, and then with help I made my way backward. I knew that in the "Bavarian Gulch" about a quarter hour away there was a bandaging station, to which the company's wounded had been taken repeatedly.

There it looked bad—the whole deep gully was full of wounded men with wounds of all kinds. While a doctor worked on a couple of badly wounded men, several medics tried to help as well as they could. For me they could do nothing more; the bandage, by now crusted with blood, was firmly in place, but I was given a painkiller. "Right now we're not taking anyone away; the Ivans are close behind us," one of the overworked medics told me.

After a time, two assault guns appeared at the entrance to the gulch—they had opened the road to the rear, it was said, and "they're going back again; slightly wounded and whoever else wants to can climb aboard." I had meanwhile met a man of my company with an arm wound, and we wanted to go; comrades who were already aboard helped us up onto the assault gun, and the trip began, with rattling chains, bumping and thumping until I and surely many others could have cried with pain. At least no enemies were to be seen or sensed. Finally the two fully occupied iron "means of transport" stopped, one of the crewmen pointed at a somewhat distant cave in a quarry to the side and said, "there is the main bandaging station." Then they turned around and rolled back toward the front.

So a small procession of wounded, dirty and weary men, supporting each other and dragging themselves forward, made its way to where help waited. But just halfway there, a medic ran toward us waving his arms wildly and kept screaming, "Everybody turn around—full to overflowing—no more room." After I asked about an injection for tetanus, he only shrugged his shoulders: "Nothing left, Herr Leutnant, we scarcely have anything for the badly wounded."

No, there was nothing for us here. While most of the men sat down on the spot, I limped, using a stick taken from a bush and supported by by arm-wounded comrade, back to the road. There we had luck, for a truck coming back from the front took us along to a few houses, from one of which a Red Cross flag hung. It was a lone medical support point, where a medical Feldwebel with two helpers accepted us amiably and hospitably as it began to get dark. At least he could give tetanus injections, put on new bandages and even provide a straw bed. When he cleaned my shot wound somewhat, he was not satisfied. "It's swelling and turning color, needs surgery soon," was his diagnosis.

On the next day we traveled on, along with several wounded who had arrived meanwhile, on the straw-filled rear bed of a truck, and around 1:00 PM we reached another HV station that was located at a farm on top of a hill. Before the main entrance there was already a long line of soldiers with bandaged heads, arms and legs, leaning on sticks or lying on carriers on the ground, waiting patiently. A suppressed whining and gasping could barely be heard. Then it was my turn, a medical NCO took my information, and I was just about ready when a medic came from inside with a bucket from which an arm stuck. Then I was inside, where a pair of doctors worked at two tables. Trash and bloody bandage scraps lay on the floor, pools of blood, the doctors with red-spotted white aprons . . . My trousers were removed, I lay on a table and breathed the odor of ether. When I woke up, I lay on straw out in a big tent on the warm, sunny 8th of May, in a long row of freshly bandaged men. When a "Sani" gave me something to drink and hung a wounded tag on me, he reported, "It went well. It was high time—a lot of dirt and pus came out." I was not to stay here long. While new patients kept coming in—no wonder in these days of heavy fighting—ambulances brought us down the hill and past Varenikovskaya to a ferry slip on the Kuban, where we got on big barges. Then it was off across the wide river to Temryuk on the Black Sea narrows, where we were unloaded and we "lying" patients were taken to a sort of recovery home in the city. There was no medical treatment, but there was food to eat. As we were told, a voyage over the narrows was to be prepared first.

May 9—in the morning an Oberarzt made short visits and assigned us to transport. Around noon, a big bus picked us up and took us to the harbor in a long medical column. Mighty ferries, small warships and cutters lay at the long pier. One of the big ferries swallowed up most of the arrivals, for whom there were enough straw bags and blankets. Late in the afternoon, when everything was full, the rear gates closed and the trip began. Without danger or trouble, we traveled through the darkness of night.

On the morning of May 10 we arrived at Kerch in Crimea. Without a pause, we were loaded into a makeshift hospital train in the harbor area, with wooden shelves and straw, and the train rattled across Crimea.

Arriving at Nikolaiev that day, we made a three-day intermediate stop there. A big military hospital took us in. After we were first funneled through basement rooms where they washed us and took our uniforms for delousing, we went stark naked into a big bright bandaging room for new bandaging. "Simple flesh wound," said a staff doctor, "but the wound needs further treatment." "Capable of transport," one of the other doctors noted.

On May 11 I lay in a wonderful bed, getting the best care and treatment, also from Red Cross nurses, and rode with many other wounded men in a nice clean comfortable hospital train toward our homeland.

"Bravo, Doctor"

Around Easter of 1944, most of the I./"G", under the command of Regimental Commander Hans Dorr and part of a strengthened battle group, disembarked from a transport train for a relief attack on the city of Kovel. Kovel was surrounded by the Russians, and General Gille commanded the defenses in the city.

The chief of the I./"G" had likewise arrived from the station with the rest of the battalion a few hours before the attack was to begin, and received the command to attack with [p. 67] the men who had just arrived, mainly members of the 1st Company, along the railway line in the direction of Kovel.

On Easter Sunday this battle group, with light snow falling, went out over a long rise of ground to attack the—according to air observation—only lightly occupied railroad causeway. The battalion's troop doctor, Oberarzt Dr. St., had joined the battle group.

After several hundred meters, as the falling snow grew heavier and heavier, the spearhead reached a swampy patch of woods and received the enemy's first, as yet unaimed fire. The rest of the battle group moved forward into the woods, and we all sought cover against the defensive fire, which was growing heavier. The swampy floor of the forest was under water, it was cold and the damned snow fell relentlessly. Whoever hit the ground was immediately soaked to the skin.

The enemy fire from handguns, fired blindly into the swampy woods, became very unpleasant because of the many oblique shots. The first men who were wounded were happy to know that the doctor and a few "Sanis" were with them. The Russians, who had established themselves firmly on the railroad causeway, could not be seen, although we heard their shots clearly from 80 to 100 meters away. We also fired into the area, more "on suspicion" and to content ourselves. It was certainly not a "heave-ho attack".

Meanwhile, the whole battle group—about 120 men—had come into the swampy woods, looked for cover, and cursed because there was none.

Then the enemy began to use grenade launchers, and now it became very unpleasant. The young, inexperienced replacements got more and more nervous and began to move backward already. The driving snow let up, and with it, the sight limitation ended. The Oberarzt and his medics had a lot to do by now. The grenades detonated in the crowns of the meager swamp trees and did a lot of damage. Several wounded men, with fresh white bandages, set out toward the rear. Meanwhile, men were calling for the doctor from all sides; the grenade-launcher fire had done quite some harm. Through the thin trees we could be seen more clearly now, and the rifle fire became more precise.

The doctor with his bandage case sprang from tree trunk to tree trunk, fell into the water, shook himself cursing, and treated our men despite the cold, wet conditions and the enemy fire.

The terrain rose a bit toward the railroad line, and was covered with light clumps of bushes. Carefully we moved forward a bit farther, and after several meters we were at least not in the water any more. The doctor remained behind and went on with his work. We tried to use aimed fire to give him a little protection. More and more men were wounded.

Meanwhile it had cleared up completely, and there was no cover at hand. The Russians could clearly see our Oberarzt at his work, since he did not try to take cover, but just helped wherever he could. Standing up, he ran from one wounded man to another.

To our amazement, the enemy suddenly stopped shooting, and one of the Red Army men shouted for all of us to hear, "Bravo Doctor, bravo Doctor!"

Dr. St. sent the wounded back by troops, and not one of them was shot at.

After he had treated them all, he was finally given the order by the battle-group leader to go back with the last wounded, which he did—obviously relieved.

We all rejoiced with him when, some time later, he received the German Cross in gold.

His brave service at the railroad line near Kovel was one of the deeds that resulted in this high honor.

Just Got Away...

In the morning haze—it was 5:00 on March 5, 1944, near Ryshanovka—we recognized a large number of Russian infantrymen in front of our position. I, Obergrefrite Karl Emmert, sprang up to the heavy machine-gun position and could see that they were some 50 to 70 meters ahead of our line. I informed Company Chief Röll of this at once and then raced back to my bunker. I took hand grenades and ammunition and hurried back to the heavy machine gun; from there I wanted to go farther, to the Bausch Group at the left. But there was as yet no ditch leading to this group; I could only get there across open country, with about 40 meters that I had to cover. The heavy MG fired, giving me protection, and I ran over there as fast as I could.

The Bausch Group had no losses to report up to that time. A heavy fire whizzed over our heads here in the foremost line. Machine Gunner Döringer let me know that his machine gun was not working any more; it was clogged with dirt. I shared the hand grenades and talked with Bausch about the situation. Döringer worked on his machine gun and raised his head too far above his cover. A shot to the head ended his young life; he fell to the floor of his machine-gun position, gasping, until he bled to death. Nobody could help him; his wound was fatal. Bent over, I ran slowly back to the ditch, had a quick look over the brush, and took a shot in my right shoulder. The blood trickled through my uniform, and I could no longer move my arm. My messenger, Haller, stood near me and immediately bandaged my wound temporarily. The bullet had gone through my right arm. I felt bad, went into the group bunker and lay down of the fresh straw. After a few minutes I became aware of what a situation I was in. If the Russians broke through and overpowered us, I was a goner.

I got up, went back to the ditch, and made the decision to run back over the open area. Three times I pushed myself up over the rim of the ditch, and every time the Russians covered the spot with fire. I almost lost my courage; then I sprang out of the ditch and ran for my life to the heavy machine gun and farther back to the company troop bunker. Here I realized that I had run back at just the right time, for the enemy's big attack had begun, tanks rolled over the group's positions and destroyed all life. They took no prisoners; beyond that, no movement was possible. The company troop bunker filled up with wounded men, bringing the saddest reports to me. The number of those who were still alive grew smaller and smaller. The tanks destroyed everything ahead of them; the heavy machine gun was crushed too, and Oberjäger Engelhardt died of a shot to the head. Hans Baier and Winkler, who were with me in the morning, also died, Winkler of a head wound and Baier from a direct hit by a grenade launcher. Both had a strong will to live; we were still talking of it in the morning.

The battle ahead went on into the afternoon; the situation became hopeless; now everybody just thought of saving his own life. Our Oberleutnant Röll fired at the Russians with his machine pistol from the bunker entrance. A tank noticed this and drove up to our bunker, but it held. In this driving maneuver its left track slid into the bunker entrance. Now we were trapped, there was no longer a way out. The tank tried with all its might to get loose, trying to move forward and then backward. The bunker was full of all kinds of noise, along with exhaust gas that was blown right in at us. We almost choked; the wounded began to scream, afraid they would die. The movement of the tracks made a hole above the right side of the entrance; we could see the sky again. The tank now gave up its hopeless attempts to get loose and shut off its motor. Its left side had sunk deep into the entrance. Now we would have killed everybody who was in the bunker, for there was a hollow charge in the bunker. We attached this to the bottom of the tank and pulled the trigger cord, but thank God, the charge did not explode. One can imagine what would have happened if the charge had blown its way inside the tank. We heard the footsteps of the tank crew, but otherwise they were quiet, fortunately for us.

A group of seven or eight slightly wounded men crawled up under the tank's tracks and got out; the badly wounded men remained below. Nobody could help them any more; they probably all died there. Now we sought cover under the tank, so that nobody could see us from ahead. But we could not stay there indefinitely if we wanted to save ourselves; the situation was too dangerous. So I was the first who crawled back to a drainage ditch that ran in the direction of the village. It was frozen, and the brush offered a little cover. But the ice didn't hold any more; I broke through and got all wet. That was all the same to me; I got up and stamped through the snow, as fast as possible, back to the village. Five of my comrades had followed me, and we saw other survivors running back. We found a little cover in a ditch. Now the enemy saw us and fired its tank guns at us. Obergefreite Nierer of the supply train, running beside me, was hit on the left side of his face by a shell fragment. He stopped and fell slowly, killed immediately. A big wound gaped in his cheek, and his last breath turned to fog in the air.

I reached the village and found a bandaging station, where I was treated quickly. The doctor operated on the worst cases, other wounded were loaded onto horsedrawn wagons and taken away. At any minute the bandaging station would have to close, for nobody could stop the Russians any more; in the positions ahead, everybody was dead. It was lucky for us that the enemy was busy with his own affairs for a long time; surely he too had a lot of dead and wounded. The attack from the flatlands probably cost him great losses too.

Now I ran on to the edge of town, from where a big tracked personnel carrier took me to the next medical support point.

Last Aid for the Company Chief

On June 22, 1944, the great Soviet summer offensive against the German Army Group Center began. About the attempted breakthrough from one of the many large and small Soviet pockets that came into being in the rapid enemy breakthroughs northwest of Vitebsk in the area of the 3rd Panzer Army in June 1944, a member of Army Engineer Battalion 505 reported:

". . . The storm troopers were not followed by any medics, for that no logner made sense. They could not take the badly wounded men along. One's comrade to the left or right functioned as a medic when the wounds were slight. If they were worse, the man had to lie there. Springing advances under enemy fire. A splinter tore up our company chief's back. Luckily, I was able to drag him into a small flat dip without being hit myself. A comrade threw me a package of bandages. I bandaged the chief as I had already bandaged many others. When the enemy fire let up somewhat, two of us dragged him into cover behind a bush, creeping and rolling, and from there back into the woods out of which we had come. The Oberleutnant was badly wounded and no longer recognized me. I don't know whether he survived the wound and imprisonment..."

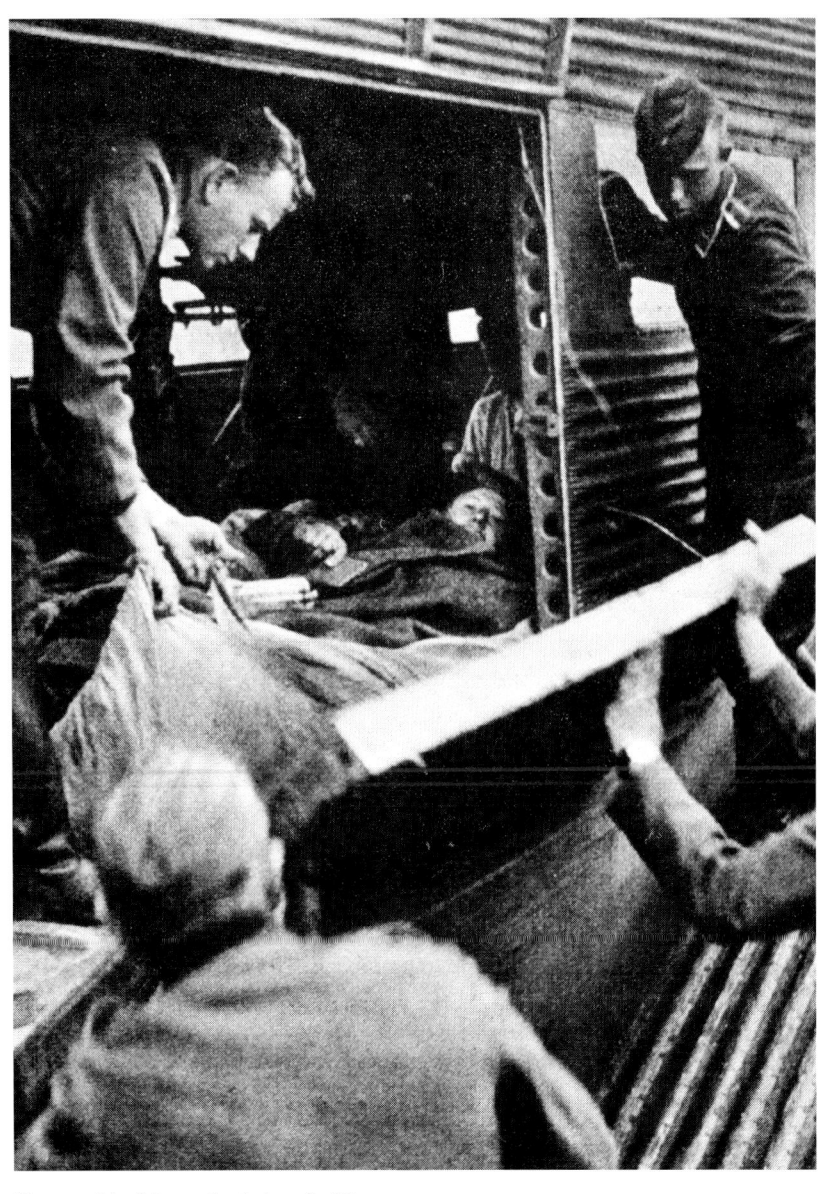

Transport for lying patients in a Ju 52.

Hopelessly Surrounded in Action

It was the battle of Stalingrad, in the course of which 220,000 men of the German 6th Army had been surrounded at the end of November 1942, and had been defeated early in February 1943. Of 91,000 (according to other sources 128,000) prisoners, only about 6000 came home. The Luftwaffe was able to fly out 24,910 wounded and sick plus several hundred specialists in Ju 52 planes from Novemver 22, 1942 to February to January 23, 1943. Nothing more is known about another thousand wounded men.

A radio report sent out by the Army toward the end of the battle said: "In the central area of the city, some 2000 untreated and starving wounded . . ." But the worst radio message came from the pocket on January 26, sent to the Army Group Don: "The situation compels us to give no more treatment to wounded and sick, so as to keep fighting troops supplied." AOK 6/Ia. This was horrifying and would have meant complete surrender even at this point.

Among many medical officers and men of the surrounded army were two widely known doctors. They were Oberarzt Dr. Reuber, whose Christmas picture "The Madonna of Stalingrad", drawn with primitive means, has since been reproduced in numerous newspapers, paintings and sculptures, etc. And Dr. Kohler, who was only released from Soviet imprisonment in 1955. After his return he received high honors from the government in Bonn for his extraordinary service to the German prisoners in Soviet camps.

After Stalingrad came 1944, the year of the great Soviet offensives and pocket battles. They began as the winter ended, when between January 2 and February 16 two German army corps (IX and XXXXII) were surrounded near Cherkassy. Again as at Demyansk, Cholm, Stalingrad, etc., the Luftwaffe sprang in to help and, with its Ju 52 planes, was able to transport out 2188 wounded, including 637 very seriously wounded. In the process, 32 planes were lost. But from February 10 on, as the premature spring thaw set in, covering the only airfield near Korssun with thick mud, no planes could land any more. When Korssum had to be abandoned three days later, some 3000 wounded who could not be taken out were left behind to surrender to the Russians, along with those who cared for them.

In the planned breakthrough on February 16, 1450 newly arrived wounded, unable to walk, had to stay behind with their doctors and medics in Chanderovka and surrender to the Red Army to save the mobile forces. Taking them along appeared to be impossible. Yet many units tried to take their wounded with them on tractors or farm wagons. Not all of them made it, though.

Soldiers who were able to escape from the encirclement reported, among other things:

When the group prepared for the breakthrough on February 16, the small town of Chanderovka became the gate of hell. The way to the readiness area led all the troops through the village on the only through street. It was the only line of march for five divisions, all the supply trains and backline services of the two enclosed corps. On the thoroughly muddy, rutted and overcrowded street we moved forward very slowly, endless columns of marching men, motorized and horsedrawn vehicles and guns pushed and shoved, bumped into each other, wedged in and got stuck. Since the enemy already had a view into the pocket and our movements could not be concealed from the enemy, directed fire

71

from the Russian artillery, ultraheavy grenade launchers and salvos of gunfire struck regularly among the stopping and slowly moving masses and caused heavy new losses. The only bridge was also under fire. Destroyed vehicles, dead horses, exploding ammunition wagons, burning trucks, dead and wounded men piled up. And new bursts of fire striking home, clouds of smoke, cries and curses, and the gasping and groaning of the badly wounded whom no one could help any more.

As the 17th of February dawned, the advancing German units had to realize to their horror that they were not, as hoped, meeting the German relief forces, but only the second Russian enclosing ring. The enemy fired all his weapons into the confused and fatigued advancing columns. Everything was mixed up, there was hopeless disorder, and any order that still existed began to break down. All leadership failed and gave up. Advancing Soviet tanks, against which the struggling masses had no defensive weapons, appeared everywhere. The enemy fire grew heavier all the time. Now the wounded men, who had been carried along on vehicles, were left alone to meet their fate. And the enemy knew no mercy or sympathy. Oberst Franz, Chief of Staff of the XXXXII. Army Corps, who survived, saw how some 15 tanks rolled through an area where a column of wagons carrying wounded men had stopped. The horses were shot down by machine guns, the wagons crushed by the tanks. There were thirty badly wounded men of the Waffen-SS "Wiking" division. Dr. Thon could only save barely a dozen. Another 140 badly wounded men, who had been taken along in tracked vehicles by the same division, were wiped out by enemy tanks west of Chandarovka; among them, Dr. Isselstein fell to the fire of a T 34 tank. And a column with wounded men of the "Wallonien"

brigade did not escape, nor did many others. For those 25,000 to 30,000 men who escaped from the pocket, reaching their own units, which formed only a weak advanced bridgehead, did not mean their complete salvation; that was waiting many kilometers farther back. After transport planes had taken out a number of the men badly wounded in the last few hours, it was still possible up to the late evening of February 18 to fly out over 1500 wounded and sick whom we had been able to bring back. Stabsarzt Dr. Königshauser and his crew worked ceaselessly at a troop bandaging station until the very last patient had been temporarily treated and sent on his way.

On March 10, the medium-sized city of Tarnopol, on the Sereth River in former southeast Poland, was declared a "fortified place", and on March 23 it was finally surrounded by the Soviets. In the constant bitter street and structure fighting, all the wounded had a bad time from the start. There was no field hospital; the wounded had to drag themselves to the bandaging stations in the dark cellars, or be brought there by comrades. The few troop doctors and their medics among the forces thrown together there wanted to help but could do little about the manifold misery. Since no supplies of medical materials came in, everything was lacking—bandages as well as medicine, ether, tetanus serum, circulatory treatments, etc. A radio message on April 4 reported 850 badly wounded men and references to their catastrophic condition.

After the commander of the fortress had ordered a last retreat into the western part of town across the river (he was killed in the process), more than 1300 men still capable of fighting moved there in the night of April 13-14. Any wounded who could still walk or limp, be supported or carried by comrades, went along. Small units remained in the eastern part of town to hold out until the badly wounded and those unable to walk, for whom there were no longer any vehicles, could be brought back. Constant heavy enemy attacks, though, forced them to give up this area in the early hours of February 15. Seven hundred badly wounded men had to be left behind, left to their fate.

In Zagrobela, the western part of town, the new badly wounded were housed in the cellars of the few buildings. Since the only outdoor well was under fire day and night, the troops suffered from a lack of drinking water, which made the suffering of the wounded even worse. In the end, their lips could merely be moistened. In addition, there was no way to bandage and treat the newly wounded.

In the end, only 55 men made their way to freedom—nothing more was ever heard of all the others or the wounded.

After Crimea had been surrounded by the Soviets in the spring of 1944 and the German 17th Army had been pushed back everywhere, the final attack on the large land and sea fortress of Sevastopol, which had been captured by te German troops despite heavy losses two years before, began on April 24. Now Fort Maxim Gorki I was one of the field hospitals in the Sevastopol area. Under its thick roofs of concrete and iron, and behind its equally mighty walls, long rows of wounded lay in the gloomy, stuffy and overfilled corridors. Whining—gasping—weeping—begging for help . . . Doctors and medical crews did what was in their power until they dropped. And new ones kept coming in, holding each other up, or were carried in. On the steep coast nearby, a trench had been dug so the badly wounded could be taken down to the water, to the piers where they were put into the boats that took them out to the big transport ships lying in the roadstead, to travel across the Black Sea to the hospitals in Romania.

Other wounded were flown out by air. The crews of the Ju 52 planes did incredible things, especially in the last days. Amid Russian searchlight beams, anti-aircraft fire and fighter planes, they came in at night, flying low, and landed on the dark landing strips, lit only by the brief flaring of lamps. Many were wrecked while landing or went up in flames before they could take off again. The ambulance drivers, who were underway to the troop bandaging stations all day and brought the wounded to the two small airfields during the night, experienced terrible things when exploding shells or grenades set the planes afire, and out of the flaring flames the screams of wounded men already aboard rang out.

In the last three days of evacuation (May 9-12), some 25,500 soldiers abd 6011 wounded were moved, despite all the difficulties, from the peninsula of Chersonnes to the Romanian harbor of Constanza.

One particular deed deserves mention: In the night of May 9-10, unshocked troops were landed by fifty Ju 52 transport planes on two nearby makeshift runways to take out wounded men. Very overloaded, sometimes with 25 to 30 patients on board, they flew back miraculously without any losses. Thus over a thousand wounded men could be rescued. In all, in the period from April 26 to May 9, 96,800 German and 40,200 Romanian soldiers, including 33,400 German and 5800 Romanian wounded, could be carried to Romania by sea. The Luftwaffe used its transport planes to fly 21,000

In the right 9th Army to the south too, two army corps were surrounded after vain attempts to break through. From the History of the 6th Infantry Division (abridged) comes this excerpt: "All the wounded were taken along, thanks to the self-sacrificing leadership of the Division Doctor, Oberstabsarzt Dr. Lorenz. The fact that all the trucks and wagons were stuck in the mud was not his fault. Dr. Lorenz shot himself after he had been shot in the pelvis, as did Dr. Schulz after an abdominal wound.

Wounded men arriving in the city of Bobruisk by June 26, briefly treated there and transported out, got out of the city safely by rail or on the road. After Bobruisk had been surrounded, the wounded from the individual bandaging stations were brought into the halfway safe but unprepared casemates of the citadel. Thousands of wounded were ultimately gathered there. They were to stay with medical personnel, since transport out was no longer possible. Of the troops who broke out up to June 29, some 15,000 men could make contact with their own relief forces. Slightly wounded men had also joined them. Many who could walk left the hospitals and joined the troops who broke out, while others dragged themselves along on crutches or even crawling on their knees, trying at all cost to avoid being taken prisoner, with a usually obvious fate. Back in Bobruisk there remained some 5000, mostly seriously wounded, many scattered troops and the city commander. Most of them lost their lives.

In the major combat lasting scarcely two weeks, the Germans lost seven corps with 28 divisions and other units, the total losses numbering some 350,000 men, though precise statistics could never be determined.

There followed the pocket battle near Brody in July 1944. With 25,000 to 30,000 men lost, only 12,000 men of the entire XIIIth Army could escape, but again, all the wounded had to be left behind.

Then the German Army once again suffered one of its worst defeats. On August 20 the Soviet offensive against the German-Romanian Army Group South Ukraine, which defended the Dniestr front from the Carpathians to the Black Sea, began with far superior forces. Here the Russian operations moved even faster than against the Army Group Center. After just a few days, the front was broken through, and while the Romanians surrendered (shortly thereafter, all of Romania went over to the Soviet Russian side), the second German 6th Army (the first had been destroyed at Stalingrad) was pushed into a gigantic pocket south of Kishniev and met its end there after futile efforts to break out. For around 20,000 men who were not yet surrounded, the word was "On your way to Pruth, which offers rescue under the sign of 'Enemies all around'." Dead tired, fought-out soldiers who had already been in unbroken combat for three days and nights, moved farther back, exhausted, bringing their wounded with them. The latter were in a miserable condition, for treatment was scarcely possible. Slightly wounded men were supported by comrades, badly wounded men lay on requisitioned farm wagons, many unconscious, many already dying.

Thousands upon thousands of fatigued, exhausted, despairing men, many wounded among them, gradually gathered on the east side of the river—but there were no bridges. While all the wounded who were taken along here had to be left behind in the end, everybody —who could—tried to reach the west shore under enemy fire, only to find out to their horror that they were on a large island in the middle of the Pruth. A survivor reported on what happened:

"The renewed enemy fire had cost great losses, we had many dead and even more newly wounded, to whom we gave particular care. I organized the gathering of bandage packages, outer clothing and shoes, which were passed on to the few doctors present or to unclothed men. Most of the doctors and medics had remained with the wounded on the east shore of the Pruth." When some of them finally reached the west bank, they were surrounded there, just as were parts of the 8th Army, also hit by the enemy offensive.

By August 29, six German army corps with 21 divisions, as well as army and corps troops, numbering some 260,000 men, had been lost.

Only some 350 men of the 6th Army and some 1200 of the 8th Army could fight their way to the new German front line in the Carpathians.

As to the fate of hundreds of thousands of German soldiers in the Army Groups Center and South Ukraine—dead, wounded, missing and captured—eternal silence remains. Only from a few who fought their way back or returned from imprisonment came a little information, a few messages. As was shown during the combat itself, it was no longer possible to transport the wounded back to a safe hinterland. Thus it was said of the 45th Infantry Division (Army Group Center): The numerous wounded were loaded primitively onto farm wagons and driven around for days, whereby many died." The Russian breakthroughs and encirclements were achieved under full air superiority and so quickly that no transport out by air was possible.

Along with the combat troops, all the divisions' medical units and other medical services were crushed, scattered, surrounded and captured. Yet doctors and medics, the personnel of the main bandaging stations and hospitals, gave their services as long as they could and helped wherever it was possible. They rescued and treated the wounded, even under the worst conditions, gave first aid to the slightly wounded, treated the badly wounded and remained with them until the Russians came. From them, too, nothing further was heard.

It can be assumed with certainty that doctors and medical personnel, providing they survived, continued to do their work, even under the worst conditions, in captivity.

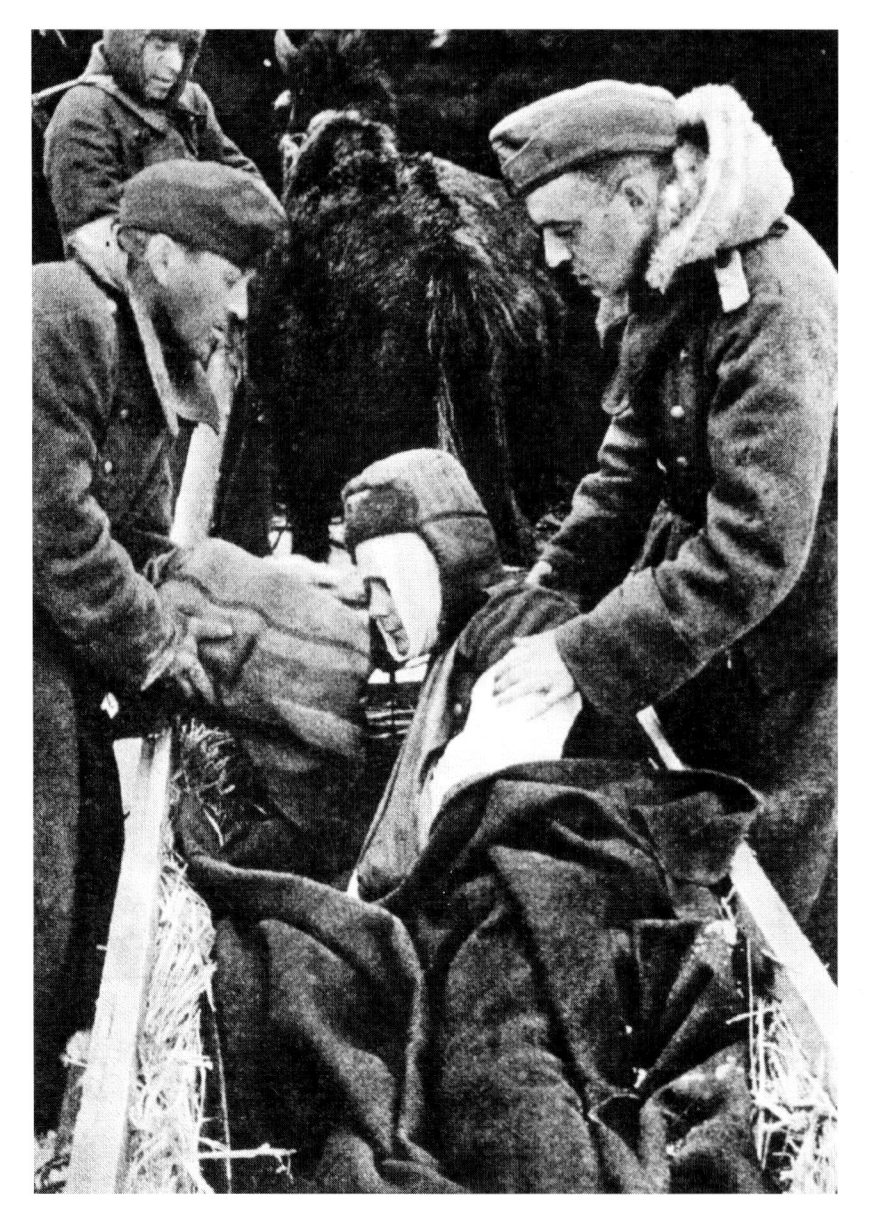

Ready to be taken to the HV station in a straw-filled horsedrawn sled.

Rescue By Sea

After the Army Group Courland was denied a further retreat by the OKW (Wehrmacht High Command) and was fully enclosed by the Soviet enemy, a similar fate threatened the 4th Army in East Prussia. Through wide and deep advances toward the Baltic coast, land connections with the Reich were more and more, and finally completely, broken, and all of East Prussia was cut off. More and more civilians fled from the Red Army to the eastern Baltic ports, in which—since no other transportation was possible any more—numerous wounded gathered. Their constantly growing numbers could no longer begin to be handled by the exhausted and fully overworked medical services, all the more so as all medical supplies were lacking and no land or air transport was available.

In this extremely critical situation, the sea transport facilities of the Wehrmacht, under their chief, Rear Admiral Engelhardt, were deployed to evacuate the ever-growing masses and bring them to safety in the west by sea before the Red Army attacked.

This transport was handled by civilian ships of all types and sizes, escorted by ships of the German Navy.

This began on January 22, 1945 with the evacuation of the most distant eastern territory of Germany, the Memel area.

Like so many other ships, the "Monte Rosa" also set out on its way to East Prussia.

At the end of 1944 the ship was rebuilt as a hospital ship in Oslo, with medical personnel and forty nurses on board. At the end of January 1945 it was suddenly ordered from Norway to the East Prussian port of Pillau, where it arrived on February 1, 1945, and immediately took well over 3000 wounded on board, and brought them to Kiel. Then it went back again.

After the Soviet U-boat "S-13" had sunk the "Wilhelm Gustloff" with some 4000 people aboard, it continued its operations from off Danzig. On February 9, at 10:15 PM Russian time, it spotted another large transporter, the "General von Steuben," a 14,660-ton ship with some 5000 people on board, escorted by torpedo boat "T 196." As Corvette Captain Marinesko prepared to launch his bow torpedoes, "T 196" unexpectedly came at the submarine and forced it to turn away.

Four hours later, Marinesko and "S-13" attacked again and fired two torpedoes at 2:50 AM. Both torpedoes struck their target. On the bridge of the "Steuben," a wall of flame shot up, while the second hit caused a tall black column of smoke to rise from the aft smokestack. Two or three minutes later there was another explosion on the ship. "T 196" hurried to help the sinking transport, covering the sea with searchlight beams and sending up flare rockets. The Russian submarine went its way toward the dark part of the horizon, increased its speed to 18 knots, and disappeared.

The "Steuben," a former passenger ship, had been armed and used to transport the wounded. On the evening of February 9 the ship had left the harbor of Pillau, loaded with some 2500 wounded, 2000 refugees and a 450-man crew. Among others, there were 30 doctors and 320 nurses on board. In its sinking, great numbers of people died of undercooling in the water. In all, 600 were saved, by "T 196," "TS 1" and one U-boat. Franz Huber, who survived the sinking, recorded his impressions as follows:

."..At Fischhausen near Pillau in Samland (East Prussia), I was struck twice on the side and back of my head by grenade-launcher fire. At the time of my wounding, I was sitting in a motorcycle sidecar, and on account of the grenade-launcher fire, the driver ran into a tree at 80 kph. From this I suffered an extremely severe loss of blood from my lower body. With these wounds I was delivered to the field hospital in Pillau and given medical treatment there. On February 9 we were taken to the "Steuben" by ambulances at night. I had a high fever and almost unbearable pains. At home in Bavaria I had had no chance to get acquainted with big ships. Thus the ship, with its dimensions, seemed like a small city to me. I was taken inside the ship and heard from my comrades that I was in the former dayroom of the "Steuben." The mattresses lay on the floor very close together, so that there was space for very many wounded men. In the dayroom there were almost exclusively head wounds.

During the trip, I went to the toilet and tried for the first time to wash the seven-day-old blood off my face, rid myself of dirt and dust, and afterward I had the feeling that I was considerably healthier. I lay down again but could not get to sleep, since there was fearful groaning and whining around me, and I also noticed how the nurses stayed longer with one patient or another, then covered him up again and said another one had died. Around midnight I fell asleep and was awakened by a terrible disturbance, around 12:50 AM on February 10.

The whole ship was shaking and trembling, and we felt as if we would burst at any minute. Everybody was crying and yelling in all the rooms. Medics and nurses stood at the doors, the ship rocked heavily back and forth. The wounded who could get up got up but immediately were flung against the walls. The other wounded slid around on their beds. We flung ourselves down, held each other, and injured ourselves even more than we were already.

I put on my uniform jacket with my life jacket over it, another comrade helped me with it. In this atmosphere of panic I tried, along with others, to reach the stairs. Now I was able to get to the upper deck, and for the first time I stood barefoot on iron and noticed how terribly cold (-12 Celsius) it was outside. It was pitch-black night, and the ship trembled.

I saw hundreds of wounded, doctors, nurses and refugees jump into the water, and I tried to reach the highest point on the ship in the hope that this part would surely sink last. I sat there in the dark a long time, alone, and heard the screams on the ship. I heard them say the Lord's Prayer in voices such as I'd seldom heard and would scarcely ever hear again. I heard the screams in the water saw that something was burning on the ship, casting silhouettes in the water from the ship. I saw numerous people squirming out of the portholes and then falling into the water. I waited and did not really know why I waited, until I heard a voice very close to me: "Now we have to jump, otherwise it's too late and we'll be sucked down."

These words convinced me, and I jumped from a height of about twenty meters and believed I was losing consciousness in the air, perhaps out of fear. I only regained full consciousness when I felt I was deep in the water. I came back up to the surface, but was right next to the ship, saw how it was leaning toward me, and thought it would bury me under itself. . ."

Franz Huber now tried with all his strength to get away. When he thought he was far enough, the suction grabbed him all the same but did not pull him under. With several hundred others, he remained on the surface. When the bubbles of air then rose from the sinking ship, gurgling and bursting, the survivors began to scream much worse than before. It was a spectacle that can never be forgotten. The last dead and wounded were washed from the deck and floated in the water. When one swam, one's hands and feet struck living and dead bodies. After some time a woman's voice called for help. Huber continued: ." . . When I got close to her, I recognized a nurse and said to her, "Come on, swim with me.' And she said, "You're going under, I have a mother and want to go home . . .'

Then I said to her, 'Either we'll both drown or we'll both survive.' She swam with me for some time, and I noticed that her strength was running out. I laid her head on my wounded body and said she should move herself and help herself so as not to get stiff. I also told her my mother's address, in case she survived.

After a time I heard cursing and arguing close by, and I thought that if they could find something to argue about, they could find rescue. Meanwhile it had become completely dark again, all the fire and light had gone out. With the nurse, I found out that a big rubber boat was nearby, a rescue boat.

The rescue boat was overfilled, and the soldiers hanging on the outside were being hit hard by the men in the boat, with rifles, pistols and hard objects. You can't imaging the drive for self-preservation any worse.

So I swam farther and more or less let myself be carried by the slight waves, still with the Red Cross nurse beside me, whom I kept telling that we'd either both try to survive or we'd both drown.

When I had already given up hope of reaching land alive, my stiff fingers bumped against something soft. At first I didn't know if it was a person, an animal or a very thick object. Very soon I had a rope in my hand that ran regularly, and I told the nurse that she should hang onto the rope and I would try to swim around the object. I found out that it was a small two-man rubber raft. As if by a miracle, this rubber boat floated in front of us, but we didn't have the strength to get into it. I tried for a long time with all my energy, until I discovered another survivor on the other side of the boat, making the same attempts. I thought if there were more trying the same thing on the other side, then I surely would find no place in this rubber boat.

The other comrade could get in, and I begged and pleaded with him to help me and the nurse, a Red Cross nurse, who had truly done a lot of good for us. But this fellow never made a sound again . . ."

After an endless time that seemed like an eternity to him, Franz Huber was also able to get into the rubber boat. He thought the other man was either fully exhausted or dead. He rested for a moment and then tried to pull the nurse into the boat. His hands were already completely stiff, and he could just hold the nurse's wrist. When, with all his strength, had lifted her chest-high out of the water, she threw both arms over her head and slipped back down. He believed he had made a mistake, tried it again and proceeded methodically to lift her up by letting himself fall backward, All in vain! He urged her to use all her strength once more, and tried it a third time. He was kneeling on the edge of the boat, and as he raised her up again, she threw herself backward, and he fell over her and headfirst into the water. Thinking that his strength was running out, he held onto the rope and was convinced there was no hope of rescue. Just as he was about to give up, he heard cries for help again and answered, "Here's a rubber boat!"

"Where's a rubber boat?" a voice called back. Out of the darkness a swimmer appeared, an Obergefreite from the Rhineland or Westphalia. He had been shot in the lung. As if that wasn't enough, when the ship sank, a heavy piece of iron had torn off two of his fingers. I told him that he could take charge of me, dead or alive, for in a short time my life would be over anyway."

The newcomer tied him fast to the rope so that he lay flat in the water, held up by his life jacket. Then he climbed over him into the boat. He pulled the nurse's dress off, made a loop of it and slid it over the nurse. Then he slung her over his knee and lifted her out of the water. With incredible strength, he finally helped Franz Huber into the boat as well.

." . . Now that the four of us were in the rubber boat, the unknown man, the Obergefreite, the nurse and I, I began to shake heavily from the cold. I thought that now, since we had all survived this long, we should all sit down and hold each other tight to raise our body heat. Superhuman things must have been done already to survive the sinking this long.

Then all four of us sat up, waited for something to happen, and hoped for rescue. After a time we saw searchlights far off on the horizon, and again it was the unknown man, a Feldwebel, as it turned out, who said the Russian submarine was coming back and would surely pick us up, and we'd be sent to a prison camp in Siberia or the Urals. Thereupon I told him we didn't need any pessimistic talk, rather we needed optimism to believe that we would survive the sinking.

Since the searchlights were pointed in the opposite direction, we assumed that she ship was very far away. Thus we were surprised when it came close to us very soon, and we called for help as loudly as we could. But the coldness didn't leave us with strong voices, because our faces had also grown stiff. We looked for our signal whistles. The searchlight was again far away. This course of events was repeated four or five times. Only at 5:30 in the morning were we picked up by the searchlight and seen from aboard the ship. It was the torpedo boat "T 196," Oberleutnant zur See Hartig in command.

I know that we used our last bit of strength to call, "Help, help, wounded!" When we then heard for the first time, "We're coming!." it was like salvation for us. Our bodies were collapsing completely. I still remember our rubber boat touching the shop, then I lost consciousness for a time . . .

With rope ladder and carrier we were pulled up onto the ship and given tea, coffee, brandy, cigarettes and everything we wanted. I no longer noticed my wound at all, but I began to feel strong pains in my legs. An Obergefreite, a young man, took charge of me and massaged me like his own brother till the sweat ran down his face. My pains in the legs got worse and worse until a doctor came and gave me an injection, so that I soon fell asleep.

We were taken by "T 196" to Kolberg and put in a hospital. I had given the Red Cross nurse my address, but I never again heard anything from her . . ."

Alois Gra wrote:

"Because of the ship's list, all kinds of boxes, tables, cupboards came sliding into the big rooms and smashed into several wounded soldiers who were lying on their mattresses. The water was already pouring into the lower decks, and an incredible panic broke out aboard the "Steuben." Shots rang out, wounded soldiers shot themselves because of the hopelessness of rescue.

The two still usable exits were stuffed in no time. Horrible scenes took place at these two locations, so that only a few were able to get out of this mass of people. I myself was one of the few, and as I fortunately came out on the upper deck, I immediately slipped and fell over the railing into the water. And now the fight for the few lifeboats began in the water. Here too there were indescribable scenes . . ."

In the open roadstead below the steep chalk cliffs near Sassmitz (on the island of Rügen) on February 27, there lay six large, overcrowded ships. Here the time-consuming transfer to smaller steamers for transport to safety on land took place, because the big ships, on account of their draught, could not get into the harbor.

Still on the evening of the 27th, the unloading had to stop, for the wind increased to Force 7. But there were still 12,000 wounded plus numerous refugees on board. Meanwhile, 22 hospital trains were sent out from Swinemünde to Sassnitz on the single-track rail line.

During the pauses in the wind, the unloading went on, but at the end of the month there were still 9000 wounded not yet landed. On the ships there was a lack of food and drinking water, and the danger of epidemics also increased. Thus the ship's doctor of the transport "Deutschland," basically an internist and just recently having been assigned to the ship that also lay in the roadstead, having arrived from Gotenhafen with 1400 wounded men, reported:

"I tried, along with two or three medical NCOs, to treat the wounded and went, as if making rounds at a hospital, from one to the next. Soon I had to recognize that the job could not be finished in this manner. In the big dining hall alone there were 600 wounded men housed. Many had not been treated for days and thus were in great need. I must also mention that we had received wounded who had not been treated yet at all (from the battles around Danzig). Many even came from Courland. Most of them were patients of abandoned field hospitals. We also had a whole station of brain-damaged men on board, who were already underway for several days. We did not have enough bandaging material, so that the old bandages had to be reused. We were also lacking medicines, particularly pain-killing drugs and opiates. Anesthetics were also wholly lacking, so that in a pinch I made up a mixture of scopolamine, eukodal and ephetonine and quickly injected it intravenously. That was an experiment that I would never have thought of doing under normal conditions, but it worked well, so that we could do many operations. As well as we could, we tried to do everything not to let the wounded men's condition get any worse. But they stayed on board longer than planned. Thus it could not be avoided that they left the ship in a worse condition than when they had arrived.

Since the strong wind sometimes reached storm force, with gusts almost like a hurricane, the unloading could only be resumed on March 4, in a diminishing southwest wind, and 2586 patients could be landed. On the evening of the next day, we could send 5500 wounded men on their way in thirteen hospital trains.

Then came an air raid, in which the destroyer "Z 28" was sunk, the small hospital ship "Robert Möhring" caught fire and 350 wounded lost their lives.

Only on March 15, after more than three weeks on board, could the last patients leave the now starving "Deutschland."

In view of all the war-caused shortages, unfortunate conditions and all the hindrances, in the period from mid-February to mid-March over 100,000 people were landed, including 26,027 wounded. All of them were taken gradually, thanks to the tireless service of the federal railways, on a single-track line into central Germany.

That's how it was in Gotenhafen and Danzig...

The last defenders in the Oxhöft battles left the West Prussian mainland on March 3, after classic departing movements, and set out on the Navy's small boats that waited in the darkness of night to take them to the peninsula of Hela. About the 9500-ton transport "Ubena," Captain Lankau reported:

"We went nearer to the point of the long peninsula of Hela and began to take on wounded. At Docks 2 and 4, naval ferries, fully loaded with wounded, came alongside. The whole operation was carried out by our naval personnel. Platforms were let down onto such a ferry by our loading crane and two wounded men were placed on each. To prevent their falling off during lifting, one of our men sat on it and it was lifted up onto the deck. Up there, every man was busy with getting the wounded below decks as fast as possible. So it went, one after another, and in no time such a ferry, which often brought up to 300 wounded, was empty. The men who could still walk came on board via rope ladders.

It should not be forgotten that we were still being fired on at that time.

It got bad after the fall of Gotenhafen. In the Oxhöft fighting, the Russians had moved 17 cm cannons into position, and they fired on every ship. There were also ceaseless attacks by aircraft. Our own Flak guns fired at whatever they could, and yet the transport of the wounded and refugees could not be interrupted. Late in the afternoon we were finally finished and headed for Copenhagen with an escort. In all, we had some 5000 people on board, including about 1200 wounded.

The "Ubena came back to Hela from Copenhagen, as did all the other ships. . . .

On March 23-24 the city of Heiligenbeil was lost.

81

On March 29 what remained of the 4th Army, pushed together on the small peninsula of Balga, crossed over the Frische Haff from there to the Frische Nehrung. The 4th Army had thus had to give up West Prussia completely. Since March 18, 10,170 soldiers, 60,285 wounded and more than 4800 civilians had been brought back over the Haff.

A soldier recalls:

."..Toward evening I was badly wounded. A horsedrawn wagon took me along torn-up streets, between tanks and tractors, to Heiligenbeil, out of which the German troops were moving under cover of darkness. All the churches and larger buildings were overfilled with wounded, nobody wanted to take us in any more. We were finally unloaded at a barracks.

During the night I was probably operated on—when I woke up in the morning, I was lying on a stretcher. Both arms and both legs were splinted, so I couldn't move—but why did they leave the stretcher standing out in the hall?

I had a powerful thirst, but nobody heard me, everybody was running around wildly. Outside a hard fight was going on. The shells were coming nearer, shaking the barracks. Wounded men crawled out of the rooms on all fours, down the halls, down the stairs—their fear was tremendous, nobody wanted to fall helpless into enemy hands.

Outside it had become quieter—my calls echoed through the empty hall—a German officer bent over me: "I am the division chaplain—we are surrounded and are about to surrender to the Russians—I'll stay with you, so will the doctors and medics."

Then a Russian officer came along—he went past me and through all the rooms.

In the morning hours, a hard battle began around the barracks. German troops pushed the enemy back with their last strength in order to rescue more of the wounded.

It was the beginning of spring. Combat boots came up the stone stairs—really, there were two medics. They stuck me in a paper sack—strange, these burial bags—carried my stretcher to the barracks yard and loaded me and others into an ambulance. A fast ride under constant fire—over the Haff to Pillau on a ferry—saved for the time being . . .

The citadel there was overfilled with wounded. Medicine and bandages ran out. The gray walls were crusted with pus. Many of the comrades had infected wounds—they groaned for several hours, were more and more quiet and then slept forever. The doctors amputated arms and legs from morning to night. Every morning a doctor went through the rooms and checked to see who absolutely needed fresh bandages. Then came a medic and wrapped toilet paper around a rag with salve on it; after a short time the paper softened.

Then we were loaded onto a small hospital ship. All the beds were taken, there were hammocks in the corridors—everything was so clean, that was good. I was bandaged properly, all my wounds were cleaned, the burning pain disappeared. A feeling of blessed comfort came over us. In the morning we were all sent to Hela. How happily we would have stayed in that comfort, but the hospital ship was to go back and pick up other comrades from Pillau.

We were transferred to the big ship "Antonio Delfino." The ship was packed with refugees and soldiers. It set out and took us to safety. We arrived in Copenhagen at noon. But we were not unloaded, one day after another passed—the Danes didn't want to take us any more.

As I was being bandaged, the nurse was crying bitterly. She had just learned that her husband, a ship's doctor, had gone down with his ship, that had left Hela after us . . ."

Captain Tretow of the railroad ferry ship "Deutschland" noted: "Of 309 wounded, 120 were very serious cases. As there was still no ship in sight, the staff doctor on board began to operate on the most serious cases. He also sewed up neck veins—I helped him with it. . . ."

Along with the great losses of the "Wilhelm Gustloff" with 4000 dead, the "General von Steuben" with 4400 dead, and the "Goya" with 5900 drowned, many small ships were also sunk. Particularly tragic was the loss of the small steamer "Neuwerk" in the Danzig Bucht on April 10. It was—not aware of recognition signals at night—fired on and torpedoed by two German speedboats and sank within a few minutes with 854 wounded and medical corpsmen on board.

Early in April, Pillau still reported 41,385 wounded; nine hospital ships and five wounded transports were underway to them.

In the first half of April, almost 82,000 refugees and 96,609 wounded were evacuated from Hela. On all the decks, in all the nooks and rooms of the overloaded ships lay and sat wounded men. On April 13 there were still 5000 wounded in Pillau-Neutief, 8000 in Pillau city, and 3000 in the rest of Samland.

Then the evacuation from the threatened Baltic coast of Mecklenburg took place.

On April 26 the Soviets marched into Stettin. To escape the growing threat of the enemy, new transport movements were necessary. Along with thousands of refugees, the wounded also had to be moved again. So all the hospital ships left Stralsund and headed for Copenhagen. The Swinemünde hospital followed with 3200 wounded on the ship "Eberhard Essberger."

On April 29, there were still 10,000 wounded in Warnemünde-Rostock, in Wismar another 10,000, in Stralsund 6500, in Greifswald 6000, in Swinemünde, though, none any more.

Despite all the difficulties and although further tonnage had to be halted for lack of fuel, incredible feats of transport were reported. From March 21 to April 10, 157,270 wounded were brought to the west, which brought special praise from the Chief of the Army General Staff.

Some of the hospital ships worthy of note were: The large hospital ship "General San Martin" (11,352 tons). in four trips, brought 12,710 wounded from Gotenhafen to Copenhagen. The small "Marburg" (1618 tons) with its capacity of 250 beds had 1500 wounded aboard on its last trip.

Another large hospital ship, the "Pretoria" (16,662 tons) made six trips from late February to late April, carrying 22,000 wounded and 3000 medical corpsmen and refugees from Gotenhafen to sassnitz or Copenhagen. The hospital ships carried some 155,000 and the wounded transport ships 148,000 patients.

In an incredible transport and rescue operation by German shipping (warships and merchant ships), 1,300,000 refugees from the Baltic ports were moved, plus wounded as follows:

—Libau	19,717
—Memel	7,000
—Königsberg	1,290
—Pillau	99,335
—Danzig	45,971
—Gotenhafen	83,460
—Hela	163,363
—Kolberg	1,915
—Swinemünde	13,323
—Stettin	900
—Warnemünde	2,092
—Stralsund	4,341
—Rostock	150
—Wismar	700

(The documented statistics may well be exceeded by the actual facts.)

This total of 443,757 wounded was achieved in an operation lasting 115 days, from January 15 to May 10, 1945, even after the war ended, with all possible ships, mostly prepared for transport in the simplest way, which brought wounded and refugees to west German or Danish harbors in safety.

And that was the end result: Including German warships, 790 vessels in all were used, 450 of them former merchant ships. Among these were 13 hospital ships and 21 wounded transporters. In addition, along with the wounded, the fleeing citizens were taken along by all the evacuation ships whenever possible.

Lost, among others, of 107 merchant ships, were four hospital ships and eight wounded transporters.

In this whole operation during the fighting in the north of the eastern front, the medical services located with the troops suffered high losses of their own and were ceaselessly overworked and left with no means of transporting the wounded out by land routes. Medical services on the ships were either scarcely at hand at all, or in small numbers in the face of the constantly growing masses of wounded. But here too, they did their best, as shown by the facts that no epidemics broke out and the death rate among the wounded—aside from the sinkings—remained low.

To The War's End

With the end of the war, the Army's medical services had reached the end of their devoted, self-sacrificing path.

Just a few more episodes from the last days might be noted:

In their hasty retreat in the direction of the Hohe Tavern, one of the columns of a medical unit was still fully disciplined and unified. In the last military order of the 2nd Panzer Army, it was said, among other things: "Army Medical Company 1/592 accompanies the retreat of the army. . . ."

Completely disregarding humanity, on the other hand, was a command of the OKW Wehrmacht command staff, signed by Generalfeldmarschall Keitel on April 22, 1945, in which it was said:

"No German city is or will be named as a hospital city. Likewise there are no medical zones. I forbid any discussion of this matter or any communication with the enemy for this purpose. This applies particularly to the medical officers."

How a medical officer together with a major, along with so many other things, nevertheless avoided a threatening catastrophe and accomplished a great deed is shown in the next example:

In the Urlau ammunition depot near Leutkirchen in the Allgäu, 10,000 tons of normal ammunition and over 20,000 tons of poison-gas ammunition were stored: blue-green and yellow-cross grenades as well as large quantities of Tabun, the newly developed nerve poison. Their explosion if the enemy came near had been expressly ordered by Hitler. Explosive charges and fuses were already mounted. The key for their activation was held by the commandant of the camp, Major Zöller. When the approaching French troops were reported as being in Leutkirch on April 27, Major Zöller agreed with the medical officer of the depot not to blow up the depot, but to surrender it. With a white flag on his car, Dr. Jung drove to meet the French troops and reported this. After all the explosive charges had been dismantled, this huge store of grenades was surrendered in orderly fashion the next day, April 28. A catastrophe of unimaginable extent had been prevented through great courage and a high sense of responsibility.

(It is believed that these great quantities of poison-gas grenades were later sunk by the French.)

Statistics, Dates, Facts

In the first war years, until the summer of 1941 (when the Russian campaign began), losses remained within bounds.

During the five-week Polish campaign from September 1 to October 6, 1939, the Army's wounded numbered 27,278, including 527 officers.

In Denmark and Norway, there were 1548 wounded in the eight weeks from April 9 to June 9, 1940, including 66 officers.

The six-week western campaign against Holland, Belgium and France, from May 10 to June 22, 1940, cost 115,299 wounded, among them 3491 officers.

In the next campaign in the Balkans the losses were fairly few. In the three weeks in Yugoslavia, from April 6 to 30, 1941, there were 1123 wounded, including 27 officers, and in Greece 3752, including 181 officers. In Crete, on the other hand, cost the paratroops and mountain riflemen in the war against the British from May 20 to 29, just over one week, 1681 wounded, including 89 officers.

For North Africa, the losses in wounded from the beginning of the campaign on February 24, 1941 to the end of that year, over ten months later, numbered 5029. including 542 officers, according to one report. The loss figures for dead, missing and wounded increased sharply since the beginning of the eastern campaign against the Red Army. From its beginning on June 22, 1941 to the end of June (barely over one week), there were 29,494 wounded, 966 of them officers. Through July 3, thus in another 72 hours, they numbered 38,809 men (1403 officers). The terrible numbers continued to grow: to the end of July 1941, in five weeks, there were already 155,073 wounded, including 5464 officers. That was more than in all the earlier campaigns combined. By the end of 1942 there were 1,511,008 wounded, 41,524 of them officers, exceeding the 1.5 million boundary. To offer just one example here, just in the conquest of Sevastopol from June 7 to July 4, 1942, there were 17,512 soldiers wounded, with 671 officers, adding up with those killed and missing to about 1/3 of the total attacking strength.

And the losses increased further, especially in the east, where the medical services became more and more overburdened.

The Army Doctor of the Army High Command reported the following numbers of wounded (officers in parentheses) from June 22, 1941 to the end of 1943:

East:	2,397,423 (62,680)
Polar Regions	40,775 (956)
Southwest (Italy)	52,338 (1,892)
Balkans	13,697 (340)
Totals	2,504,233 (65,868)

From the beginning of the war to the end of 1944, the number of wounded rose to 4,047,924, with 105,112 officers.

A final report extended from September 1, 1939 to April 26, 1945:

East:	3,992,062 (100,994)
Africa/Italy	174,734 (4,751)
West*	264,504 (7,236)

* since invasion

Balkans	70,064 (1,841)
Polar/Norway	60,515 (1,435)
Other	28,826 (593)
Totals	4,708,977 (120,416)

In four years of war, the numbers of sick were as follows:

	Field Army	Replacement Army
1939-40	2,132,765	1,463,270
1940-41	2,102,522	1,428,604
1941-42	3,280,685	1,323,219
1942-43	3,103,199	1,683,615

And just one more statistic: The 9th Army reported, from January 31 to April 20, 1945, 25,355 wounded, particularly in the Soviet breakthrough battle on the Oder in mid-April.

According to a report of the Army Doctor, at the beginning of February 1945, there were 54,679 wounded and 67,619 sick patients in field hospitals, 354,181 wounded and 214,402 sick in hospitals in Germany. (As a comparison figure, the Luftwaffe had 10,523 wounded and the Navy 4390.) Then came the end, the six-year war was over and done with.

At dawn, around 4:00 AM, on May 23, 1945, the last radio message for the OKH/Army personnel office arrived. It had been sent out shortly before midnight by General Winter in Berchtesgaden, where he led the OKW command staff. He reported 500,000 men having died of wounds, 2.03 million dead, plus some 200,000 people who died of accidents and illness.

Wounded: total 5.24 million.

Missing: 2,4 million.

Since May 2, 1945, an estimated 70,000 wounded were in Soviet and 135,000 in American hands.

The number of wounded in Germany at that time was estimated at 700,000. One number that is found in print over and over serves to show that in all there were about 52.4 wounded and sick. This inaccurate estimate is caused by the fact that of the 17,893,200 men who served in the Wehrmacht and Waffen-SS during the war, even the slightest wounds were counted, and many soldiers, mainly of the Army, were treated several times in the hospitals for wounds and illnesses—on the average, every soldier was treated three times.

While in the 1870-71 war there were 88,500 wounded, in World War I there were four million and in World War II almost six million.

And the figures break down as follows:
— 691,000 (646,000) were badly wounded
— 125,000 lost one leg
— 40,000 lost one arm
— 10,000 lost both legs
— 900 lost both arms
— 6,000 lost their eyesight
— 1,000 were crippled
— 63,000 were brain-damaged (including civilians)

These sober and terrible numbers report of destroyed lives, pain and sorrow.

As in the entire field army, the exact losses in the medical services remain uncertain. Only individual numbers are known: The losses of medical personnel of the 1st Mountain Division in Russia from June 22 to October 10, 1941 amounted to 34.6% of the medical officers and 46.1% of the medical soldiers and stretcher bearers, based on their initial strength.

From June 22 to December 31, 1941, 12.53% of the entire medical personnel of 132 divisions lost their lives.

From September 1, 1939 to June 1, 1944, 1777 of the 2170 active doctors and 20,126 doctors of the reserves were killed or died of their wounds. The number of doctors who died in captivity or in epidemic camps is also very high.

Today there stands, in the Medical Academy of the Bundeswehr in Munich, a memorial with the simple inscription:

> To the dead of the medical services
> 1939-45

Bibliography

Brustat-Naval, Fritz, "Unternehmung Rettung," Herford, Koehlers Verlagsgesellschaft, 1970.
Buchner, Alex, "Das Handbuch der deutschen Infanterie 1939-1945," Friedberg, Podzun-Pallas Verlag, 1987.
Bundesarchiv-Militärarchiv RH 28- 1/239 Tätigkeitsbericht Div. Arzt, 1. Geb. Div., Freiburg, 1995.
Busse, Helmut, "Soldaten ohne Waffen," Verlagsgemeinschaft Berg am See, 1990.
Fischer, Hubert, "Die deutschen Sanitätsdienste 1921-1945" (5 vol.), Osnabrück, Biblio-Verlag, 1982-1988.
Guth, Ekkehardt, "Sanitätswesen im Zweiten Weltkrieg," Herford-Bonn, Verlag E. S. Mittler und Sohn, 1990.
Günther, Carl M. von, "Als Arzt im 2. Weltkrieg," Reichenhall, 1986.
Hahn, Fritz, "Waffen und Geheimwaffen des deutschen Heeres 1933-1945" (Vol. 2), Koblenz, Bernhard und Graefe Verlag, 1987.
Haupt, Werner, "Das Buch der Infanterie," Friedberg, Podzun-Pallas Verlag, 1982-83.
HDv 59 "Unterrichtsbuch für Sanitätsunteroffiziere und -mannschaften" (August 12, 1939), Berlin, Verlag Mittler und Sohn, 1940.
Mueller-Hillebrand, Burghart, "Das Heer 1939-1945" (3 vol.), Frankfurt am Main, Verlag E. S. Mittler und Sohn GmbH, 1956.
Puschnig, Wolfgang, "Tagebuch vom 25. 8. 1939-10. 5. 1941, manuscript.
Ricker, Karl-Heinz, "Ein Mann verliert einen Weltkrieg," Frankfurt, 1958.
Schirmer, F. & Wiener, F., "Feldgrau," periodical news of a work cooperative, Lehrte, 1962.
Siller, Alexander, "Chronik der 1. Geb. Sanitätskompanie 101 1941-45," Reference book of the 101st Jäger Division.
Tessin, Georg, "Verbände und Truppen der deutschen Wehrmacht und Waffen-SS in Zweiten Weltkrieg 1939-1945" (14 vol.), Frankfurt and Osnabrück, 1965-1980.
Tippelskirch, Kurt von, "Geschichte des 2. Weltkrieges," Bonn, Athenaeum Verlag, 1951.
Wagenbach, Gisela, "Die Organisation des Wehrmachtssanitätswesen im Zweiten Weltkrieg."
Werthmann, Hans, Oberartz, and Willecken, Willi, Oberstabsapotheker, "Das Sanitätsgerät des Feldheeres," Munich-Berlin, J. F. Lehmanns Verlag, 1944.
Zentner/Bedürftig, "Das grosse Lexikon des 2. Weltkriegs." Munich, Südwestverlag, 1993.
Information, notes and pictures from the author's archives.

Stretcher bearers gather wounded—in the background is a dugout.

A badly wounded man is brought to a medical support point (right). The man in front obviously is carrying a medical kit.

Medical Soldiers and Medical Officers

Where there were still few wounded: medics give first aid in the French campaign.

In action with a medical canister.

A wounded man on the front lines is given first aid.

Wounded himself, the battalion doctor withdraws with the troops.

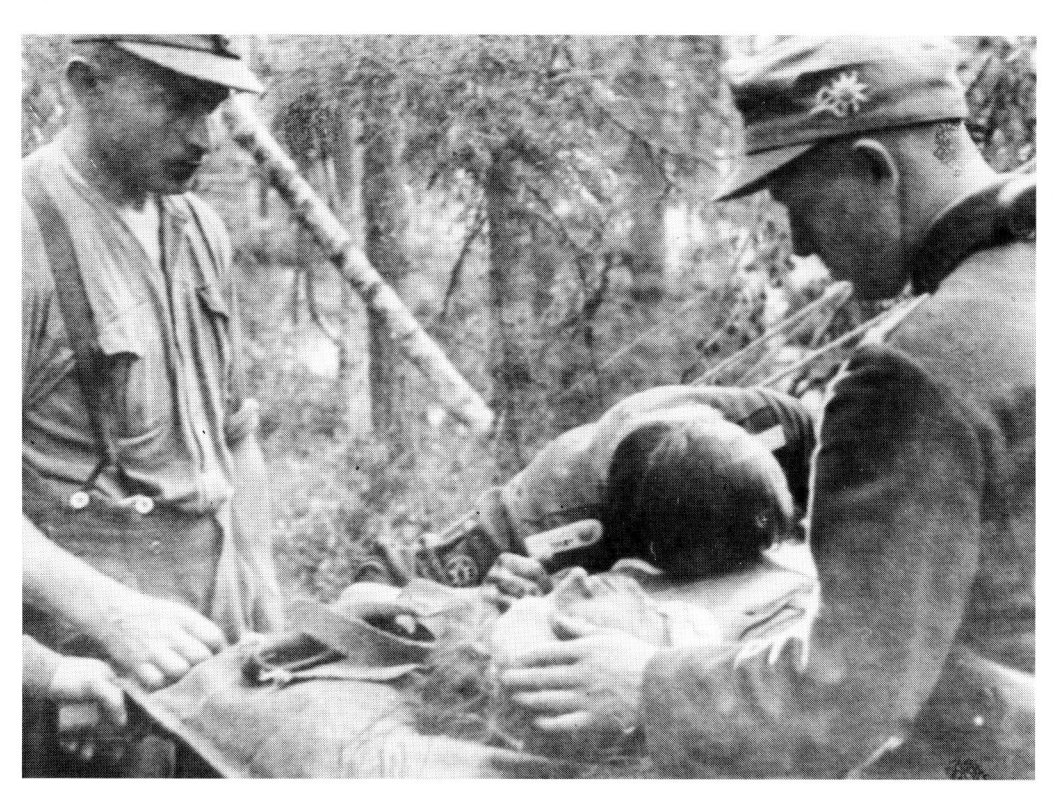

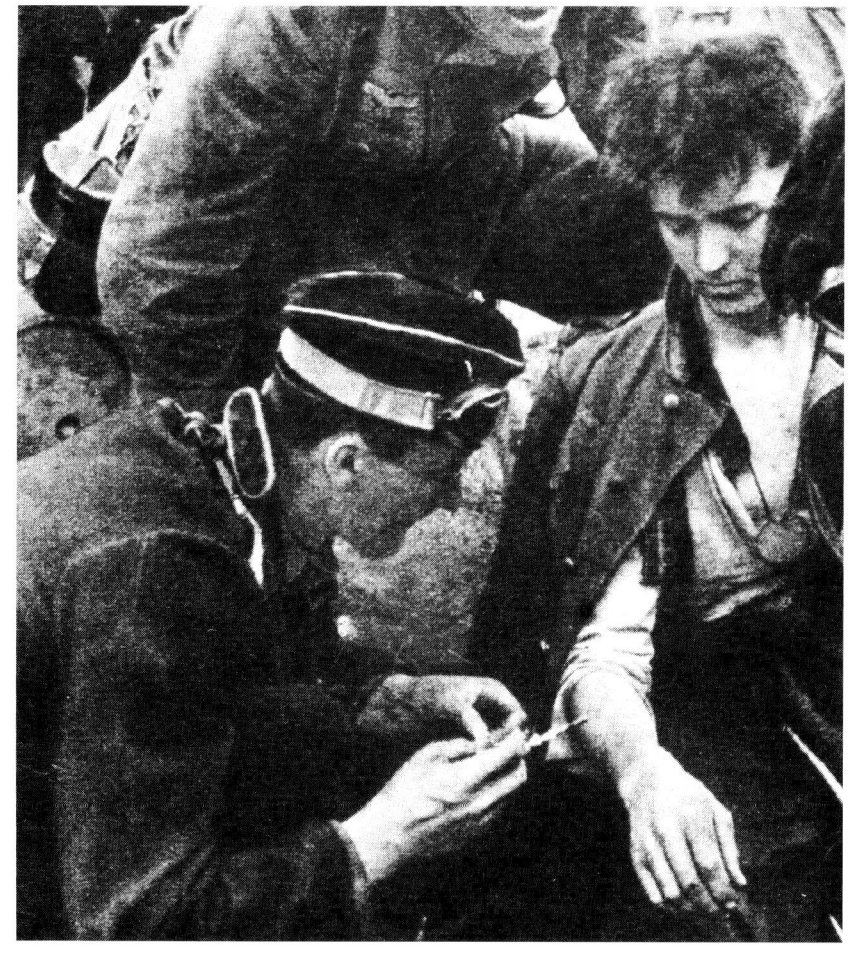

The Assitenzarzt listens: Is the heart still beating?

The chief doctor of a Panzer unit gives an injection to prevent tetanus.

A motorized medical company in the Polish campaign in 1939.

A horsedrawn medical company follows the combat troops in the French campaign in 1940.

An ambulance platoon brings men wounded in the Cretan campaign to a hospital in Athens in 1941.

A gathering place for the slightly wounded on the advance route.

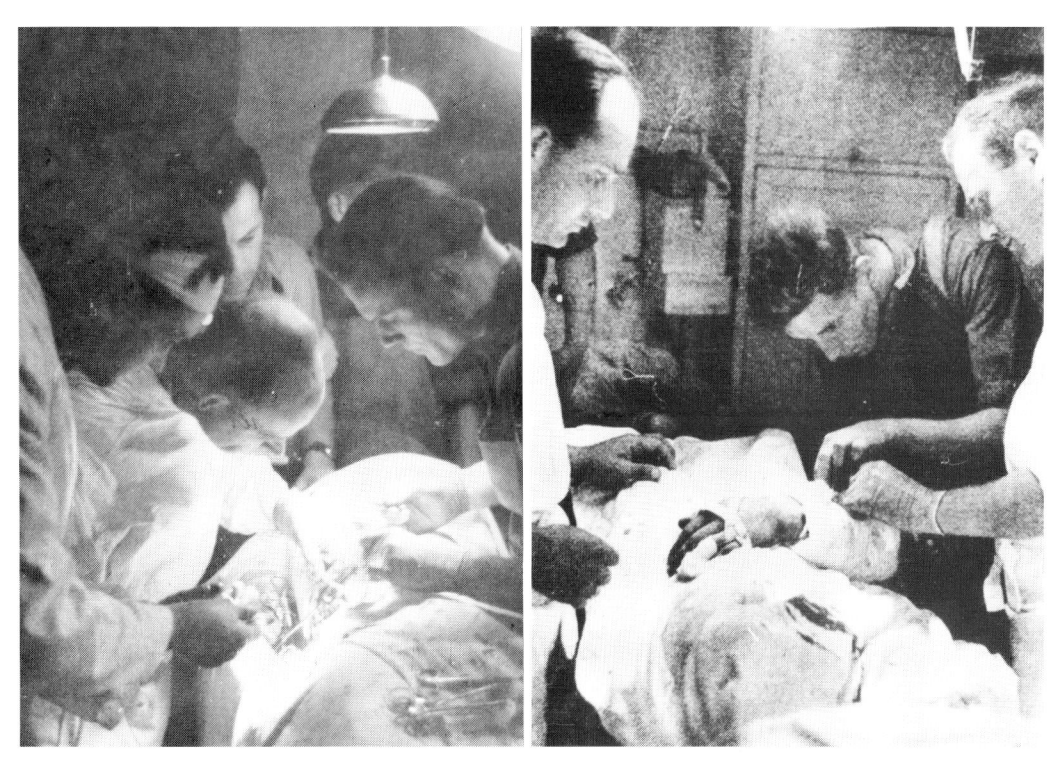

Doctors and their helpers at bandaging stations and in hospitals.

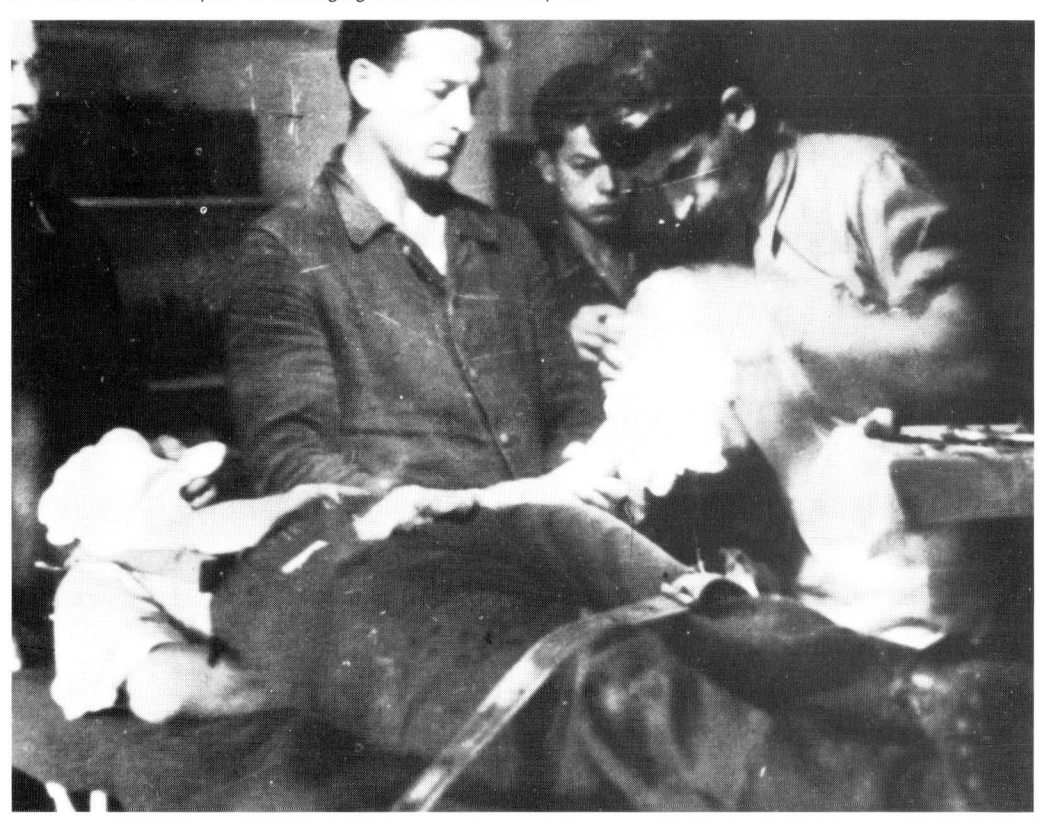

The Murafa dental station in Russia in 1941: the drill is operated by foot pedals.

A dental station north of the Arctic Circle: a patient of the SS Division "Nord" is treated.

Familiar to all the soldiers: injections to prevent all kinds of diseases.

A sauna, built by the supply-train units and gladly used in the men's free time.

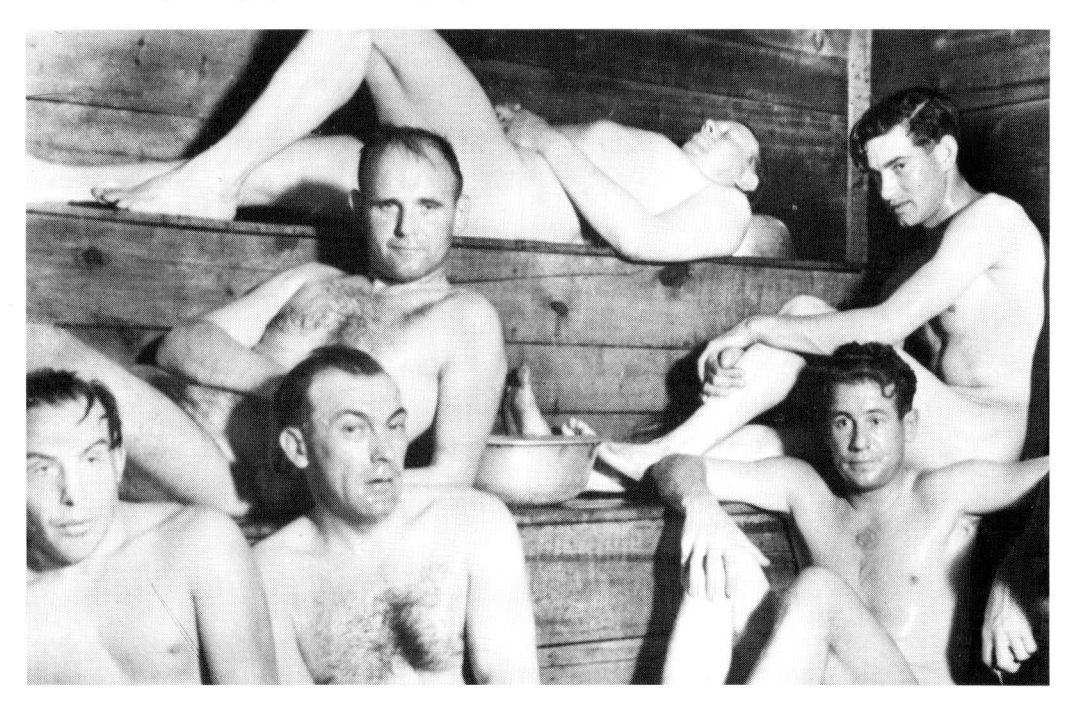

Two medical kits.

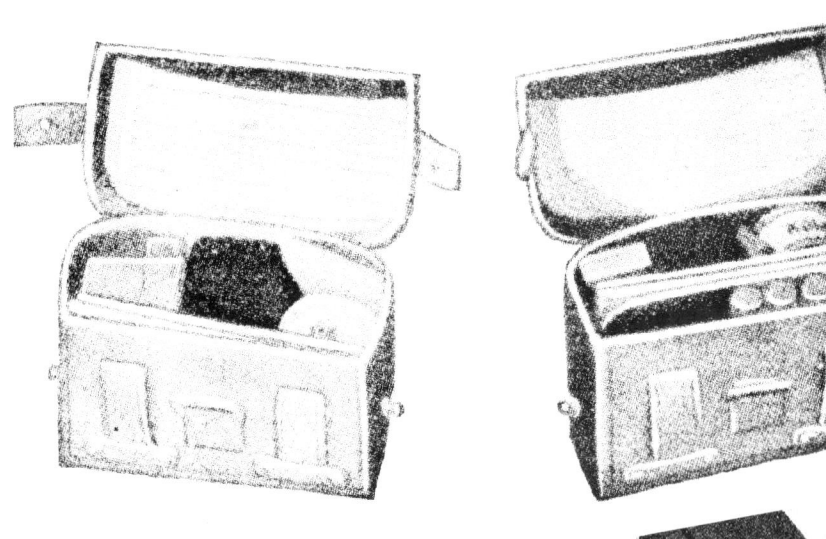

Kit I, Set a) of the troops' medical equipment.

Equipment and Kits

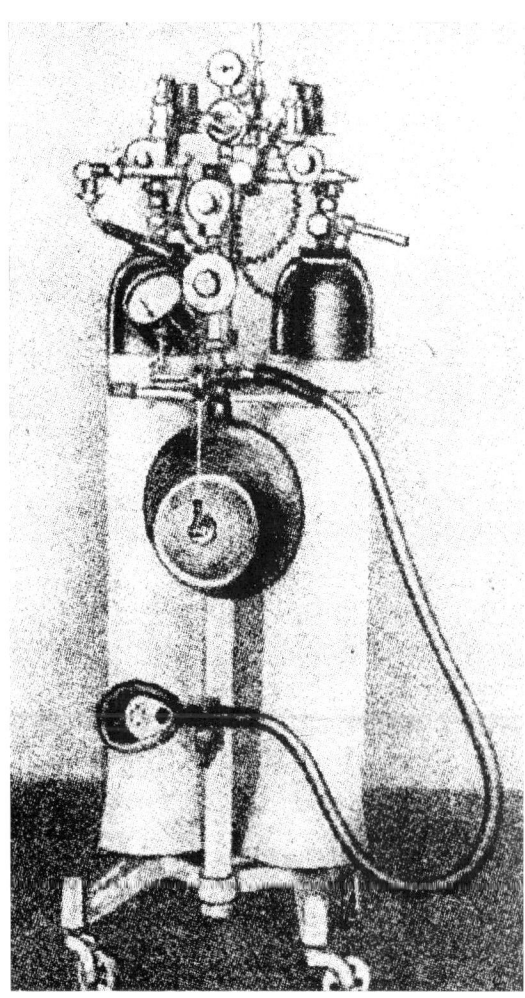

An anesthetic device.

An oxygen device.

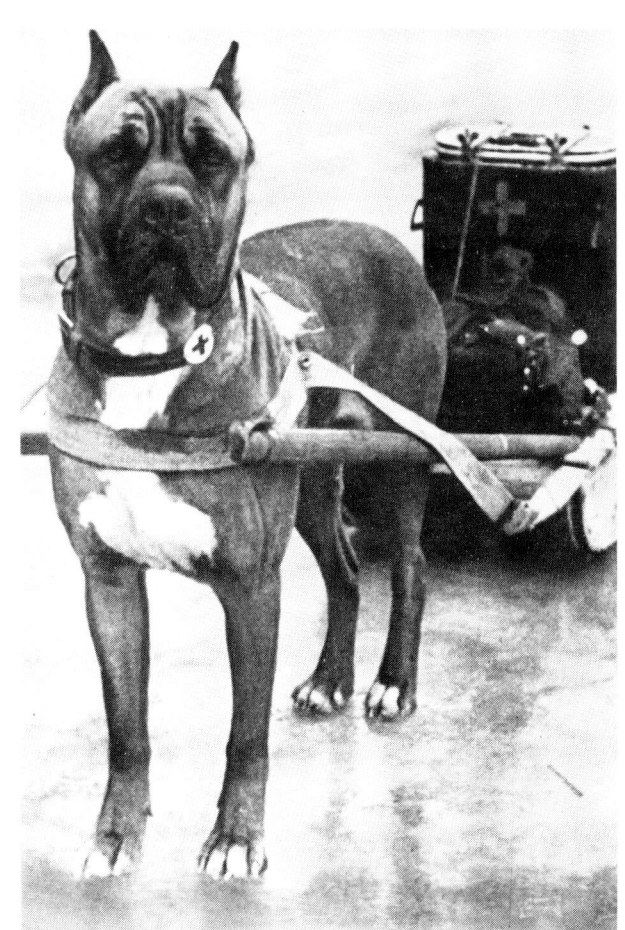

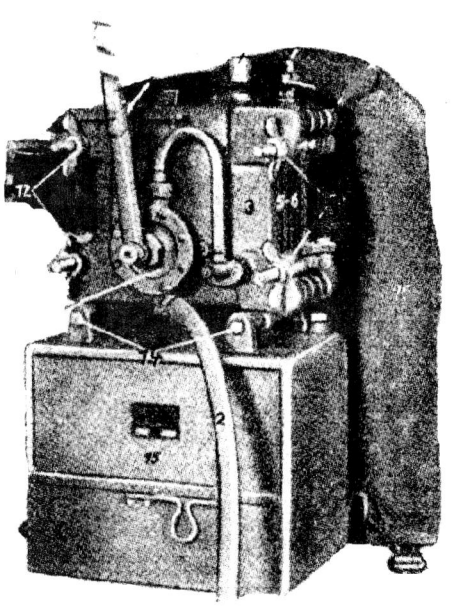

A canister filtering device.

A trained medical dog (note medical badge) pulls medical supplies on a sled (note container).

Army drinking-water preparation, with barrels and a large filtering device.

A medical tent in the western campaign in 1940.

A round tent structure made of wood, seen on the Norwegian front.

Ways and Means of Transport

Stretcher bearers make makeshift stretchers out of uniform jackets or a blanket.

The wounded soldier's tag.

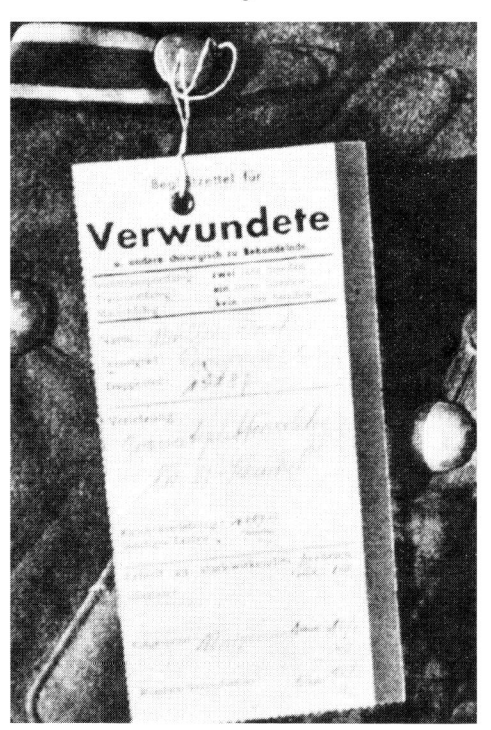

A rifle also served often as a carrier.

Medics bring wounded men through the area of fire on a carrier.

Infantrymen transport a badly wounded man with a carrying cloth (note the pierced handholds).

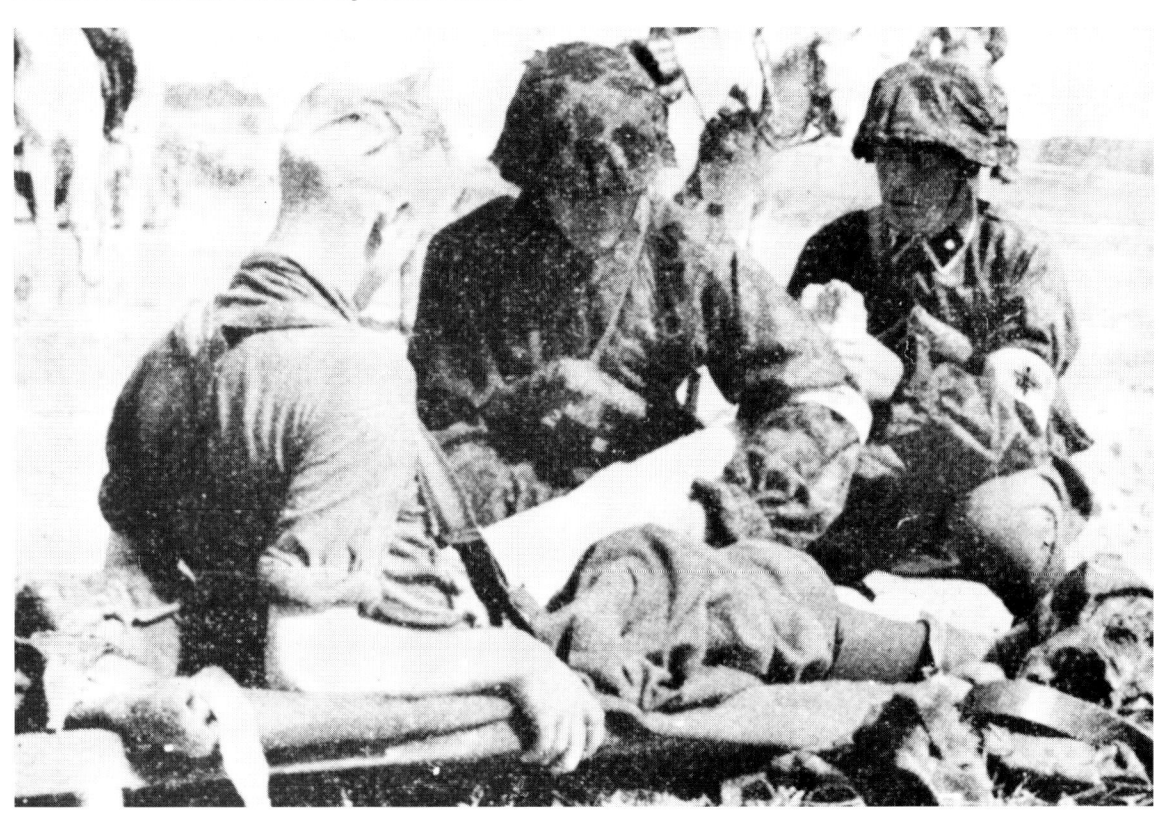

A Waffen-SS man with a wounded leg received first aid.

Transport by sled through swampy woodlands and muddy fields.

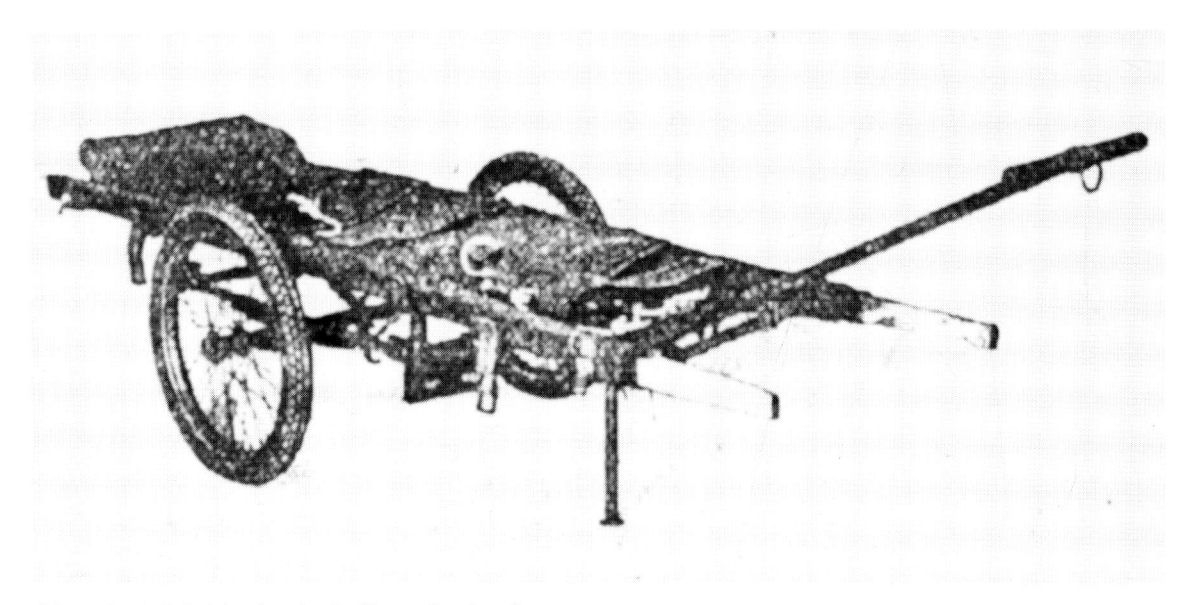

A two-wheeled stretcher handcart with a pulling handle.

A carrier device on a motorcycle's sidecar.

A new-type ambulance (Kfz. 31), made 1940-44.

A medium Schützenpanzer as an armored ambulance (Skfz 251/8).

A badly wounded man before being transported farther. The medic at front is carrying a medical kit and has the emblem with the staff of Aesculapius on his right forearm.

A badly wounded man is loaded onto a carrier padded with straw.

Wounded men are transferred from a farm wagon to a truck.

A tracked vehicle chassis with unique closed body for transporting the wounded.

A captured American Jeep is also used as a means of transport.

Soldiers pull a wounded man on a sled on the Arctic front . . .

. . . and on horsedrawn sleds. In the background is a propeller-driven medical sled vehicle.

A large medical sled with a propeller (captured in Russia).

Unique transport by cableway at the Kuban bridgehead.

Boat-shaped Akjas were especially suitable for transport in swampy areas.

A patient unable to walk is loaded into a Navy boat.

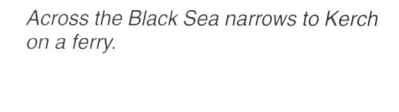

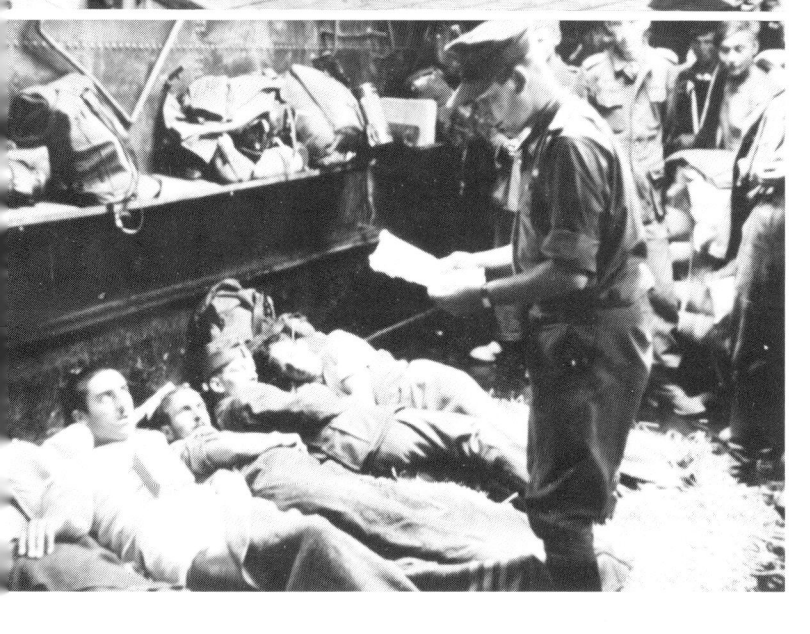

Across the Black Sea narrows to Kerch on a ferry.

A medical officer checks a patient's papers.

Loaded into a hospital train through a car's side door...

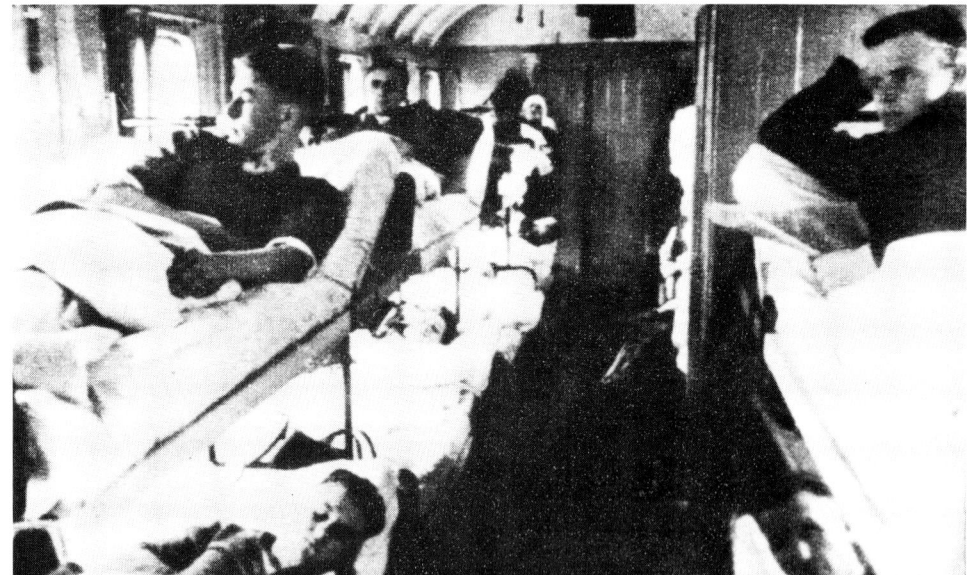

...and well settled inside the train.

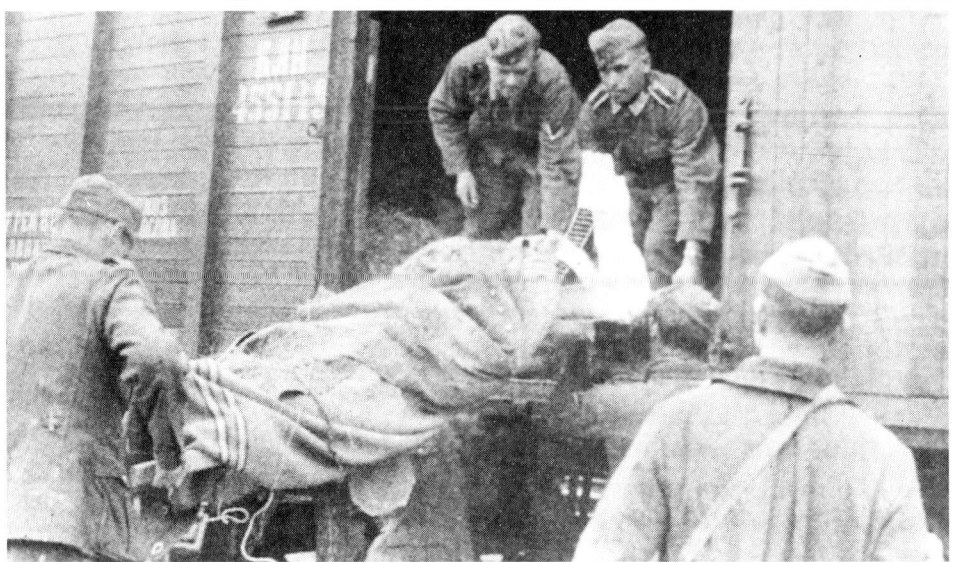

A makeshift hospital train with straw-filled cars.

A badly wounded man is unloaded from a Fieseler "Storch" plane.

Wounded men are loaded into a Ju 52 airplane...

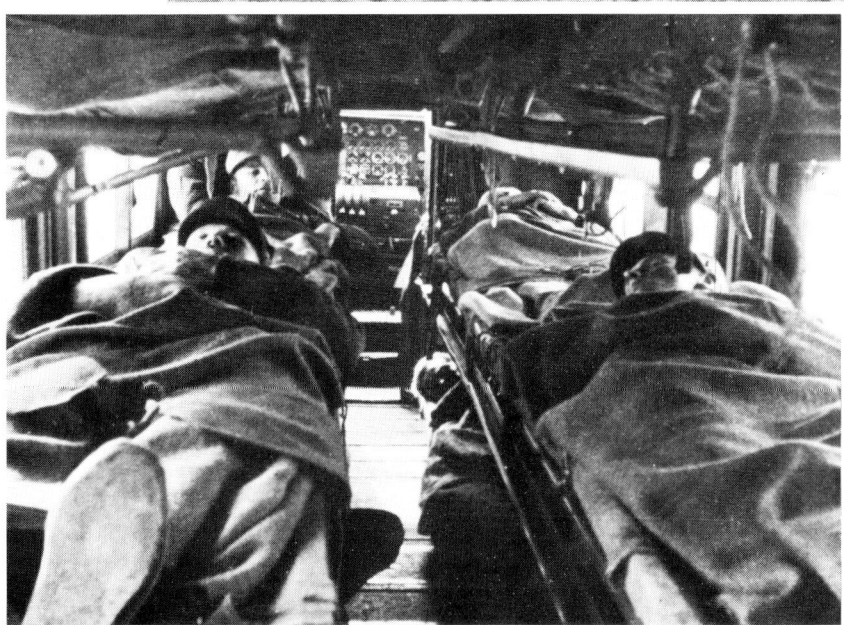

... and flown out, lying on stretchers.

A medical ambulance platoon with older-type vehicles (Kfz. 31) brings wounded men to a waiting Ju 52 in winter weather.

Patients are carried to the plane on men's backs . . .

. . . to be flown back in makeshift manner.

A gigantic Me 323 "Gigant" with opened loading area, unloading patients into ambulance for transport to a hospital in Germany.

The hospital ship "Berlin," sunk when it hit two mines.

Inside a hospital ship the commander and chief doctor are seen.

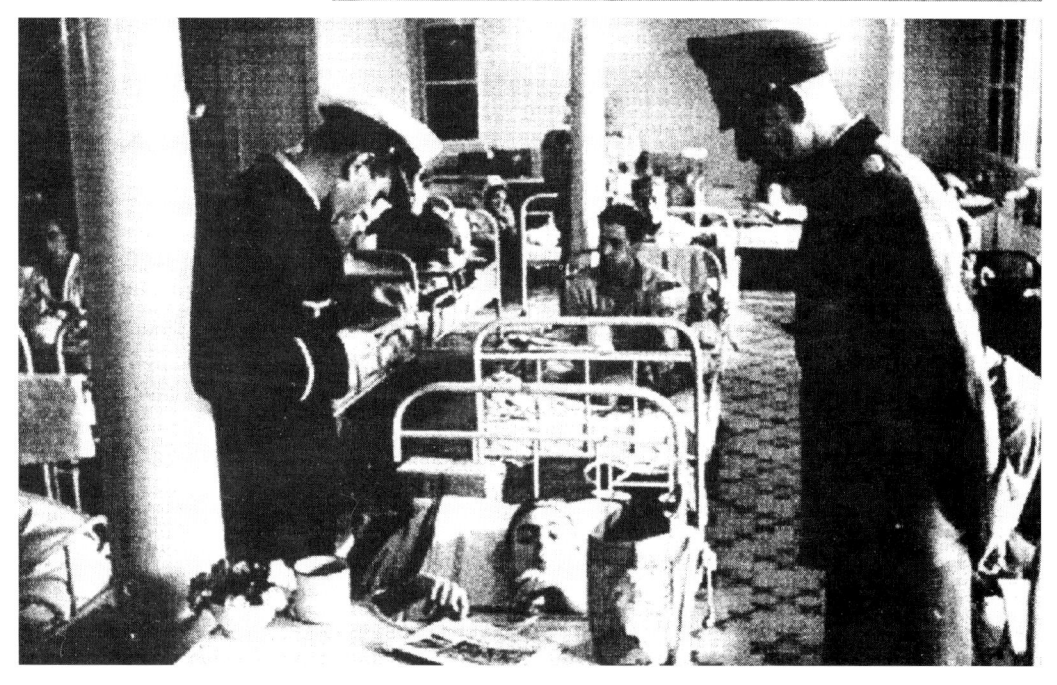

First aid up front in the trench . . .

. . . and at an armored medical vehicle.

Rescue and Treatment

Two slightly wounded men head back.

Comrades help as well as they can.

Wounded men are treated by medics at the front.

Wounded men gather in the protection of a gun (a nest of wounded) . . .   . . . and under cover behind a tank.

A sip from a bottle for a thirsty Waffen-SS man in a narrow front-line trench.

The face of a wounded soldier.

The ambulance will take the men away.

A troop bandaging station in summer—a wounded man is carried out to be transported farther...

...and in winter; a wounded man is carried in for treatment (at left is a wheel used as a gong for air-raid alarms).

At the Lavrikova bandaging station, the battalion doctor prepares patients for transport.

A crowd gathers at a bandaging station.

In an overcrowded waiting room.

After medical treatment, slightly wounded men help their badly wounded comrades in the medical tent.

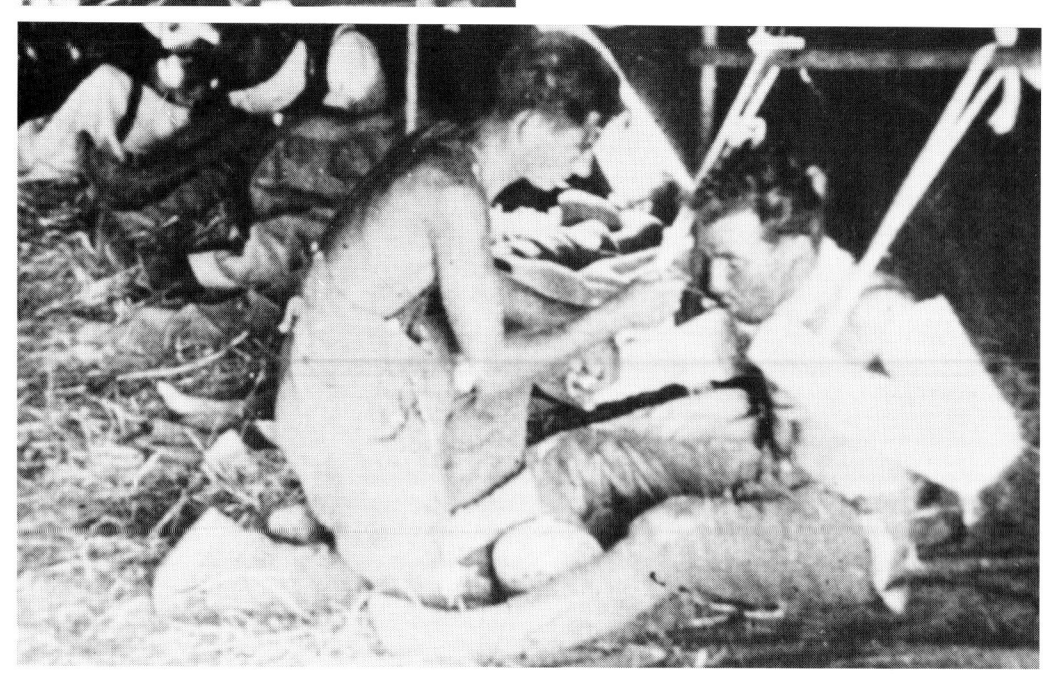

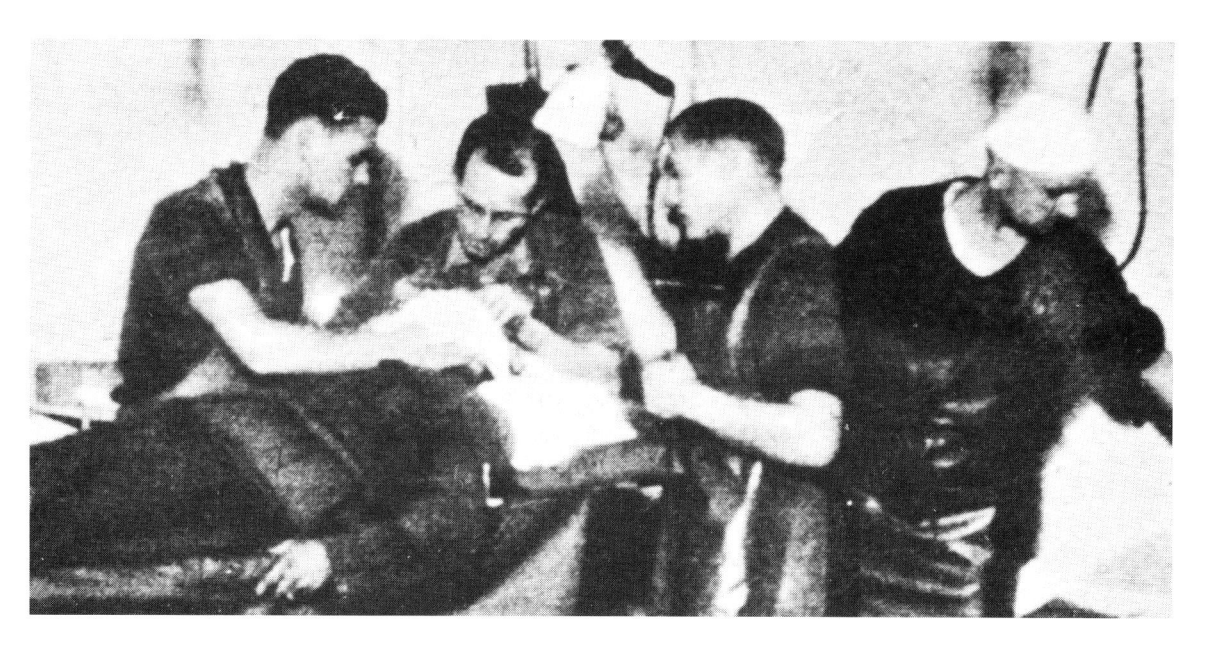

The doctors and their helpers at a bandaging station prepare for surgery.

By the light of a lantern, a doctor, busy day and night, prepares an injection

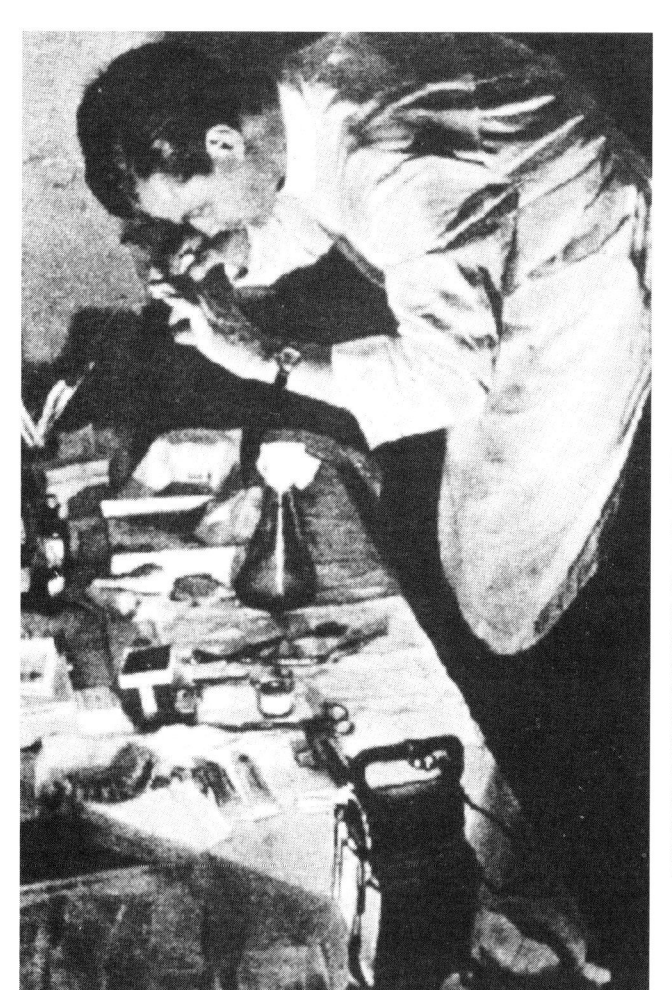

The surgeon treats the wound.

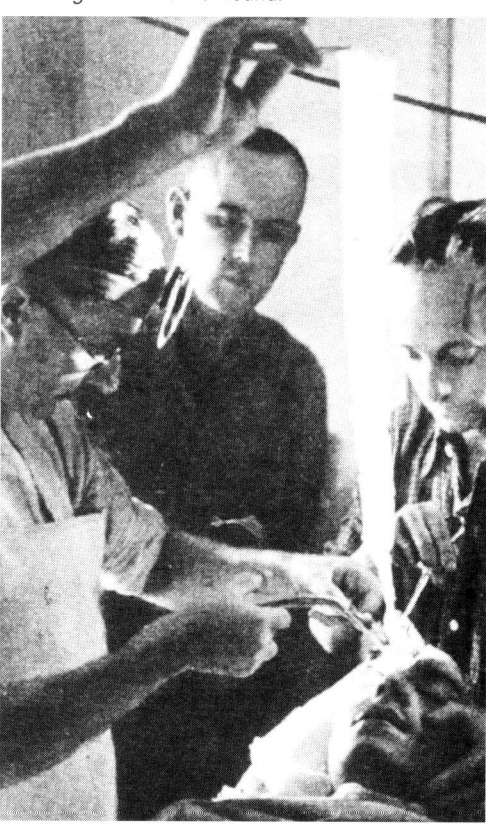

121

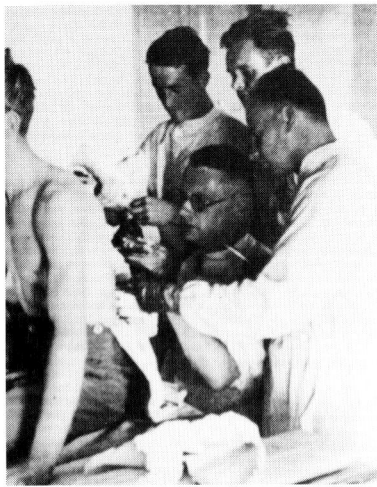

Stabsarzt Dr. Achleitner performs and operation.

The instruments are carefully sterilized by a medical Obergefreite.

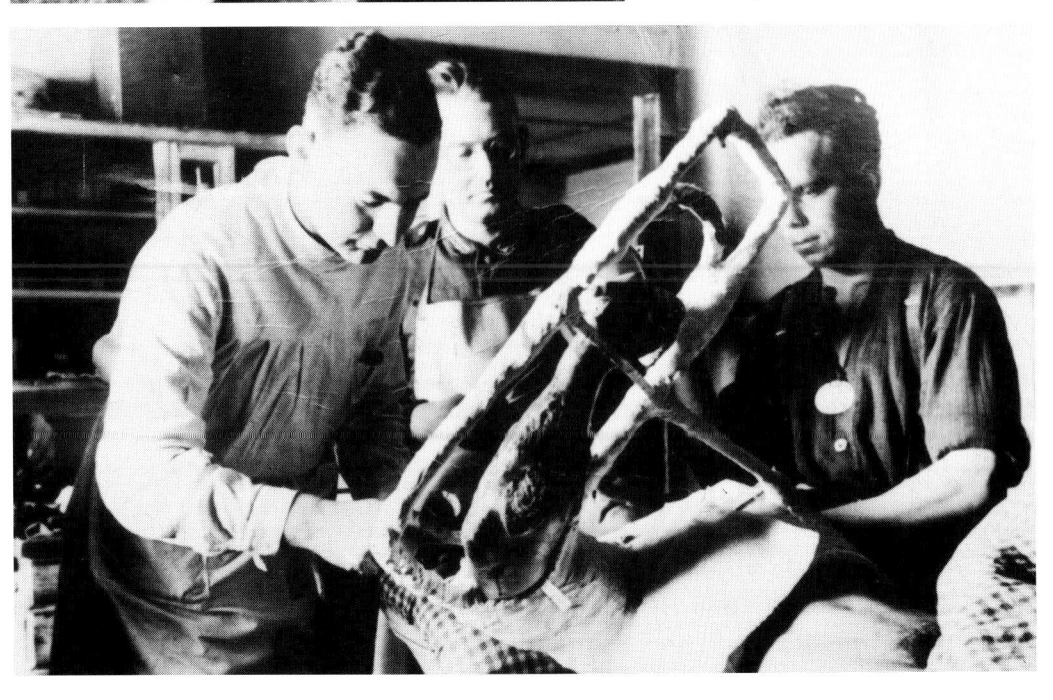

A padded splint (called "Stuka bandage" by the soldiers) is placed on a wounded arm.

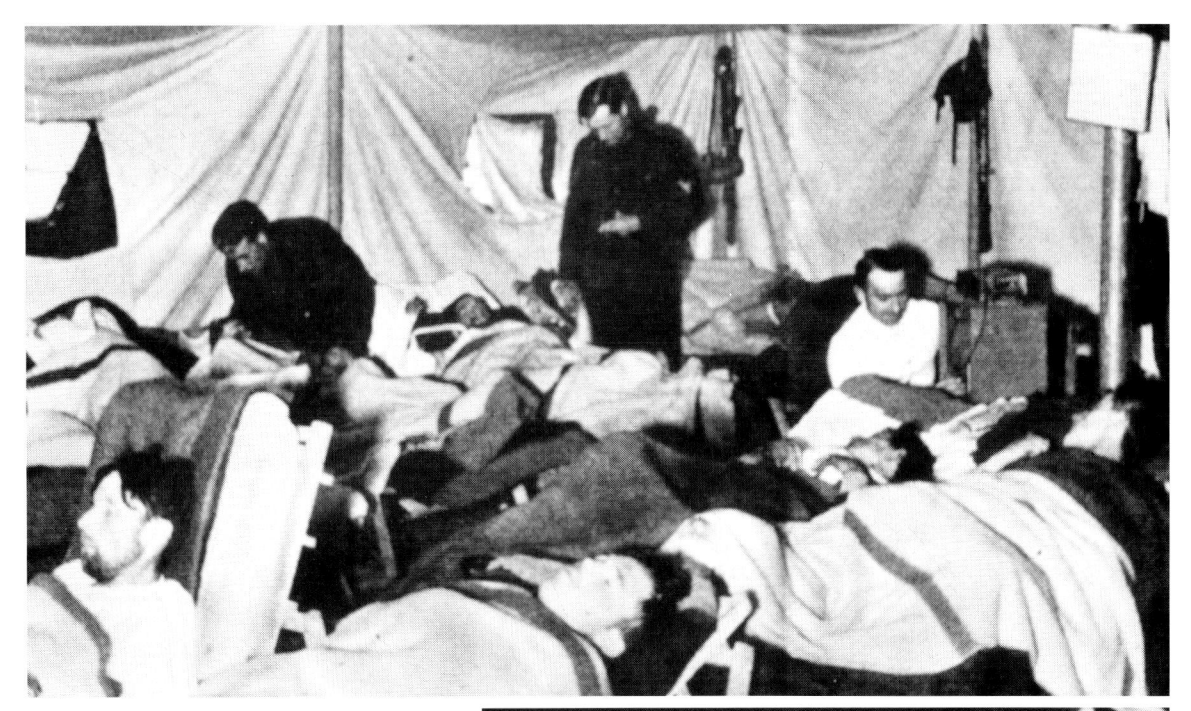

In the field hospital, every wounded man is treated. Along with the doctor (right), medical soldiers go from patient to patient, check pulse and blood pressure, give medicine and check bandages.

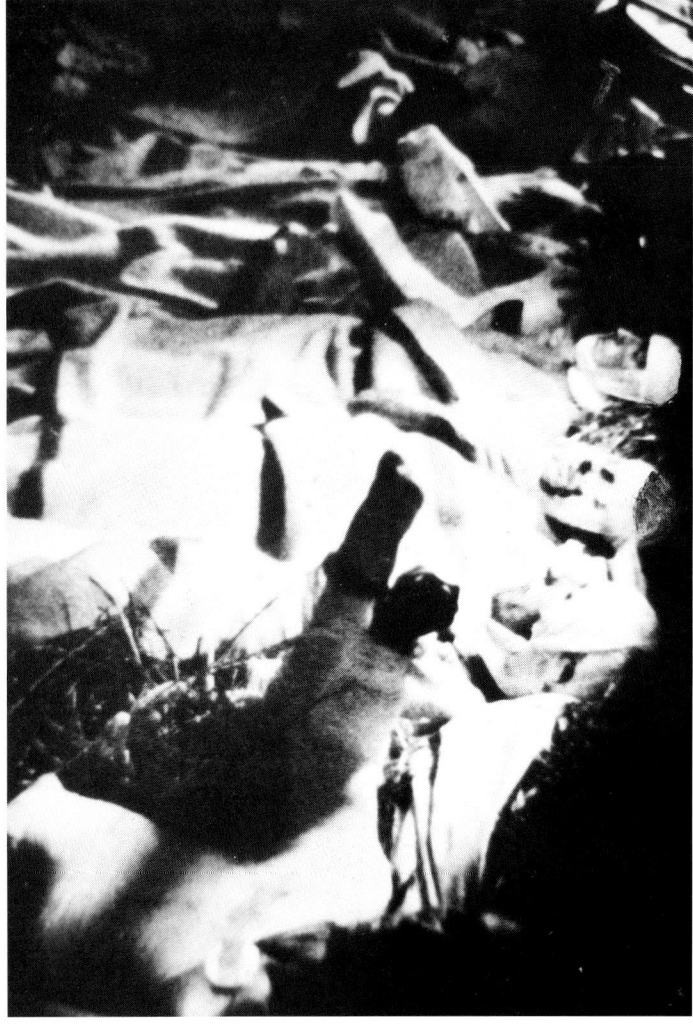

A separate department for head wounds.

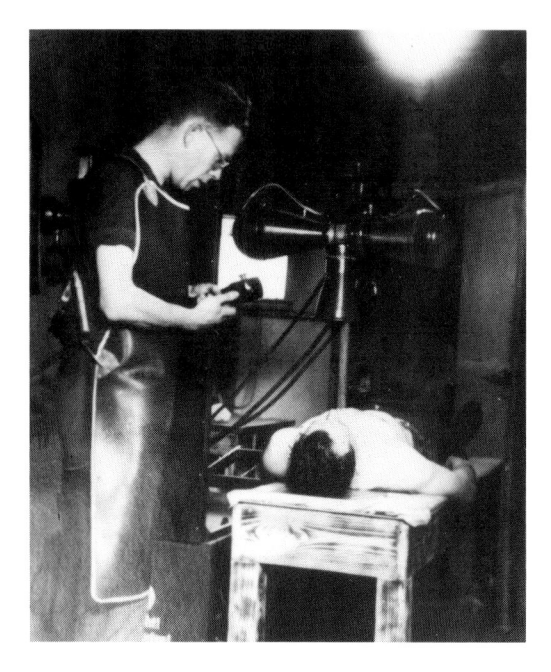

Using a field X-ray unit to determine the positions of bullets and shell fragments.

Before he decides to operate, the doctor checks the wounded man's condition. Since he has lost much blood already, he is given a saline solution.

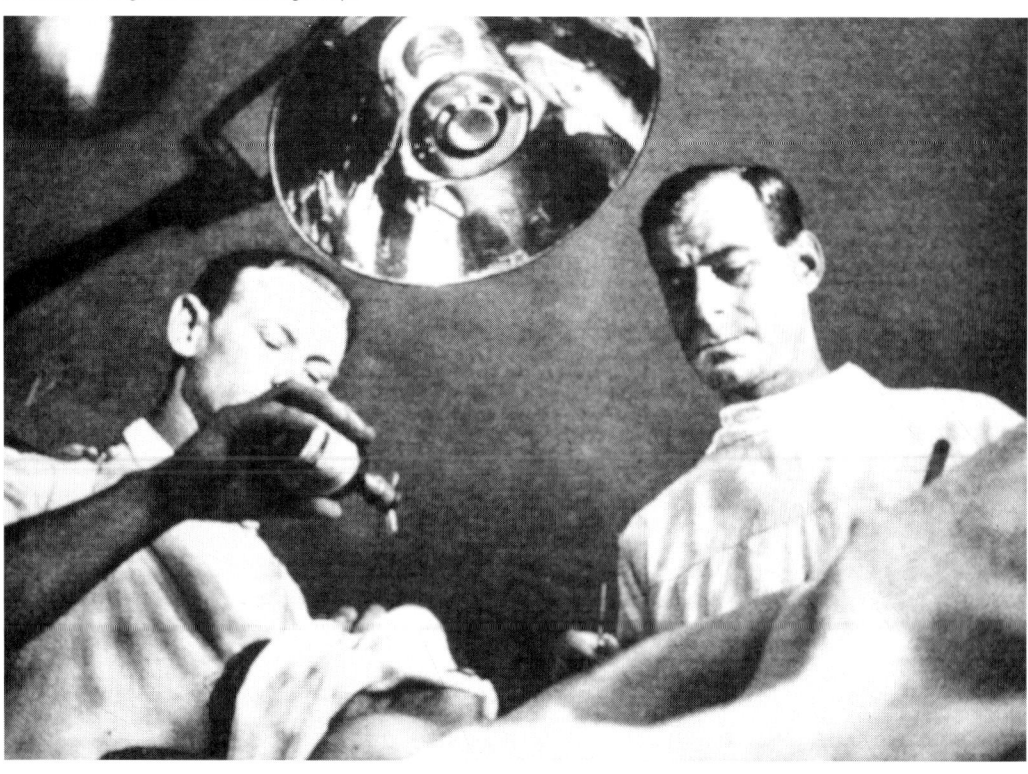

Anesthetic is given under the big lamp.

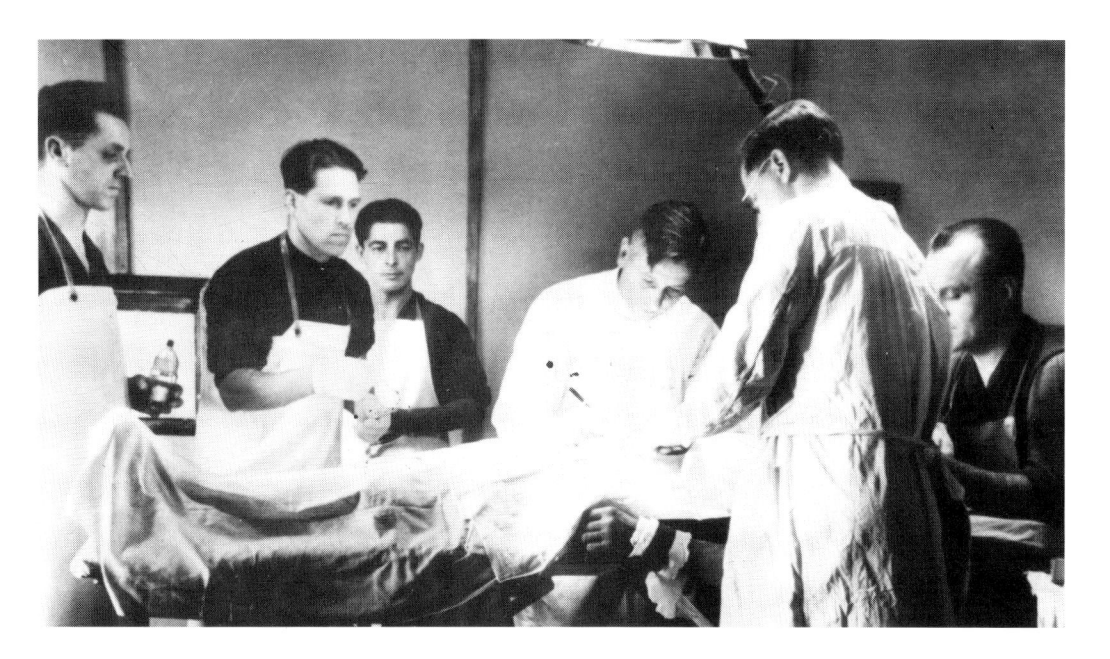

The operation begins; medics stand by to help.

In the "sound sonde" the surgeon has a device with which he can easily locate metal objects like bullets and shell fragments in the body without following the wound canal in. An X-ray also shows the approximate position. Here a shell fragment has caused a head wound.

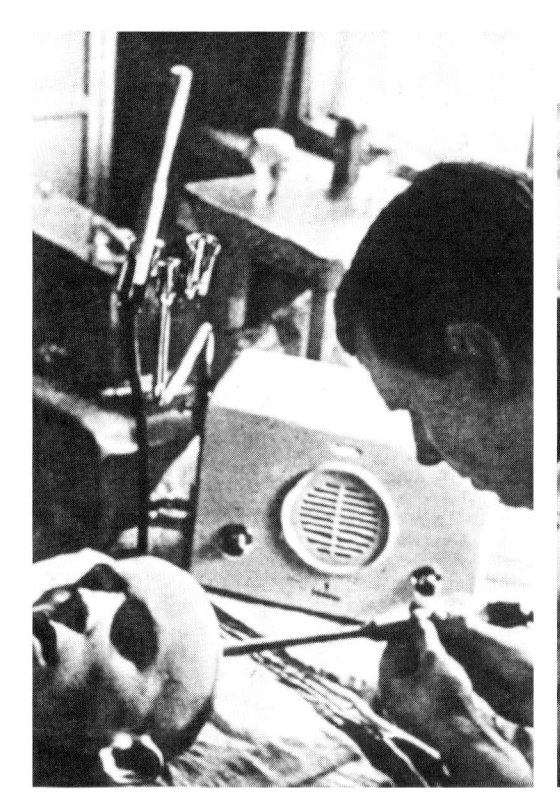

The doctor extracts the shell fragment.

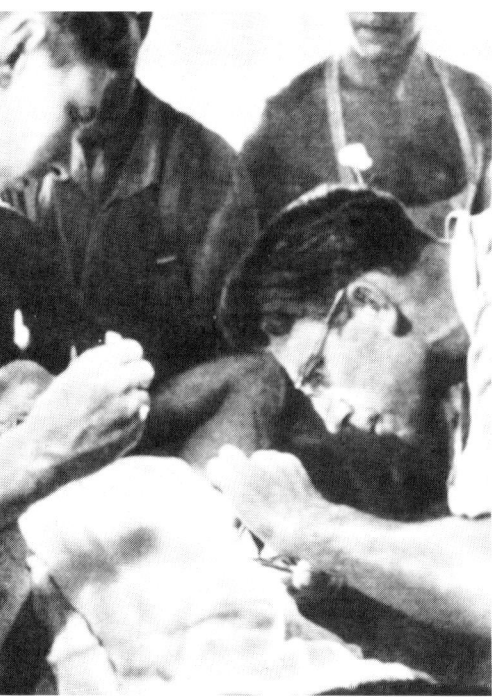

At the Kuban bridgehead in southern Russia in the spring of 1943, a slightly wounded man wades to a bandaging station.

Wounded Men on All Fronts

In the Kuban Area

A troop bandaging station in the lagoons.

Here the wounded men are transported lying on Akjas.

On the Arctic front in the far north (1941-1944), the men take pride in their homemade medical bunker.

In the Far North

A medical Feldwebel gathers a wounded man's personal effects.

In a battalion, an Assistenzarzt treats the wounded in front of the troop bandaging station made of tents.

Carrying wounded men to a field hospital may take hours.

A troop bandaging station, protected all around with high-piled blocks of snow. A medical dog and sled wait in front of it.

A nest of wounded on the front line.

Transport by Akjas pulled by reindeer.

A Fieseler "Storch" picks up wounded men in the Arctic winter.

A gathering place for the wounded in the wooded hills in 1942.

In the Caucasus

A first bandage on a shoulder wound.

A medical company with mules on the march into the mountains.

Horsedrawn vehicles take badly wounded men away.

Two horses carry a wounded man (so-called "horse stretcher").

The one-wheeled carrier in the thick woods. It was not practical, for the wheel often broke in rough country.

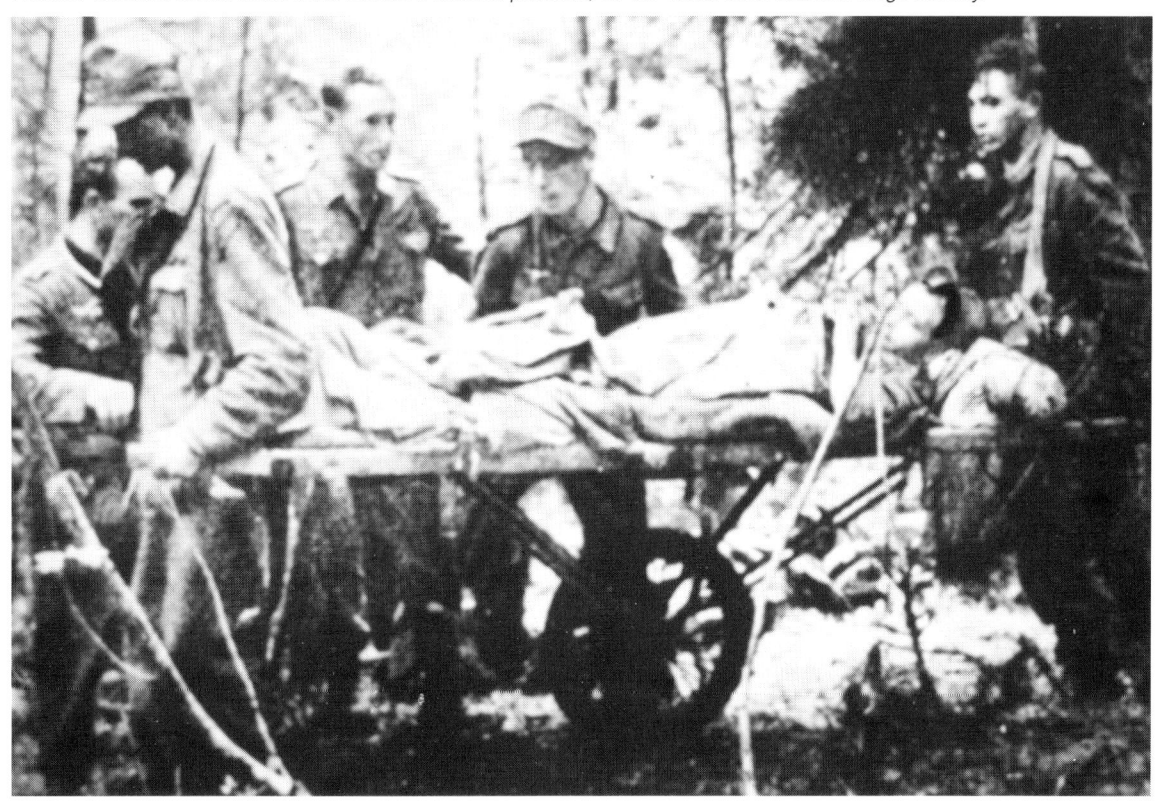

A badly wounded man is moved down a rock face on a steel cable.

Captured Russian soldiers as volunteer stretcher bearers.

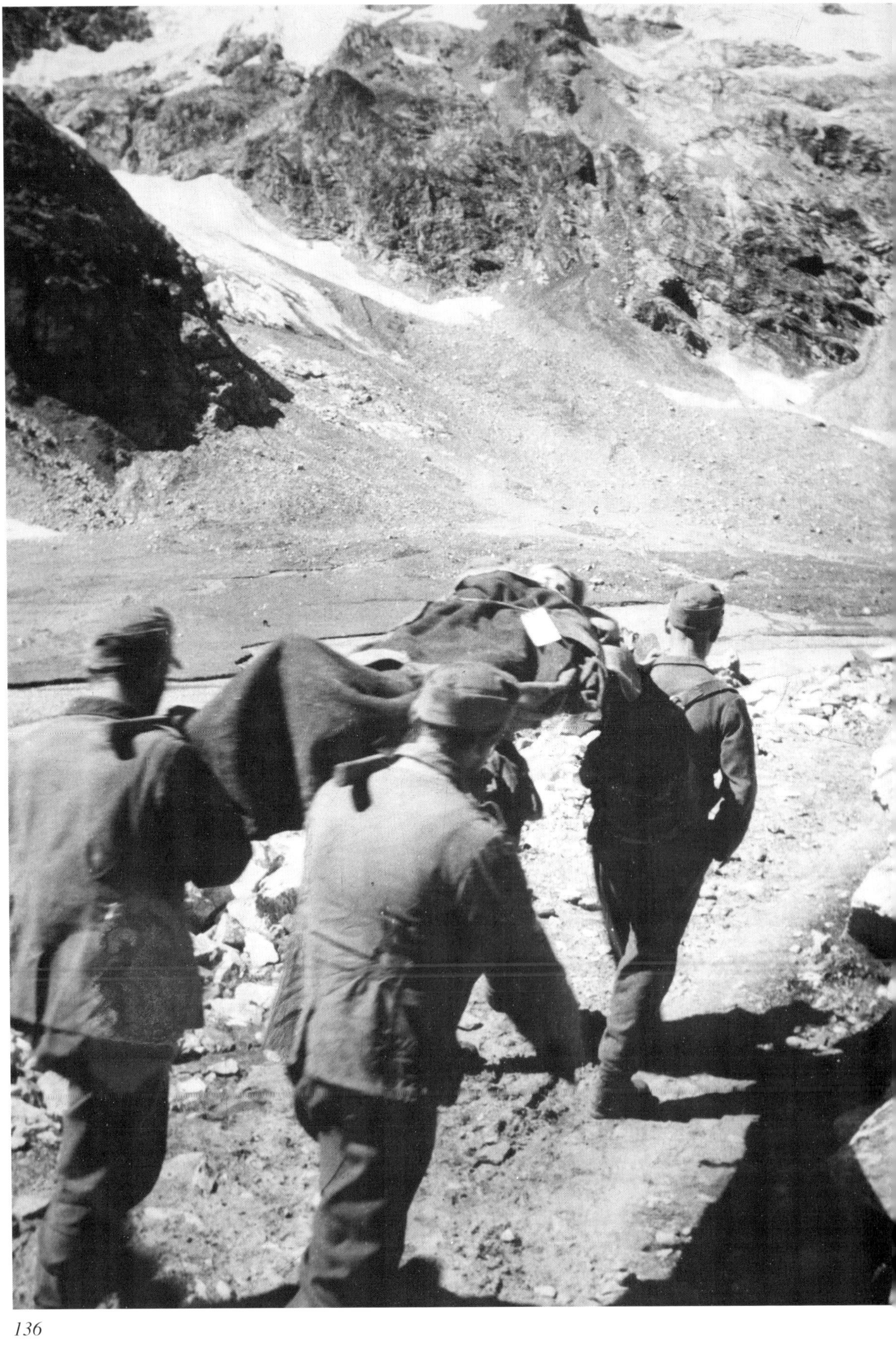

Two badly wounded men (four bearers and four substitutes per man) are carried through the Chotyu-Tau Pass, and out of the Elbrus area into the valley.

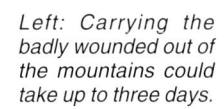

Left: Carrying the badly wounded out of the mountains could take up to three days.

Makeshift stretchers made of blankets and poles were used in the western Caucasus in the autumn of 1942.

A Fieseler "Storch" landing field in a mountain valley.

A badly wounded man is loaded into a "Storch" by the doctor and his staff. Around the patient's neck is a marker showing his blood type. The medic carries a pistol for self-defense.

Difficult rescue—out of the glacier on cables . . .

. . . and over roaring mountain streams on swaying footbridges.

This too was necessary: first aid by the troop doctor in ice and snow . . .

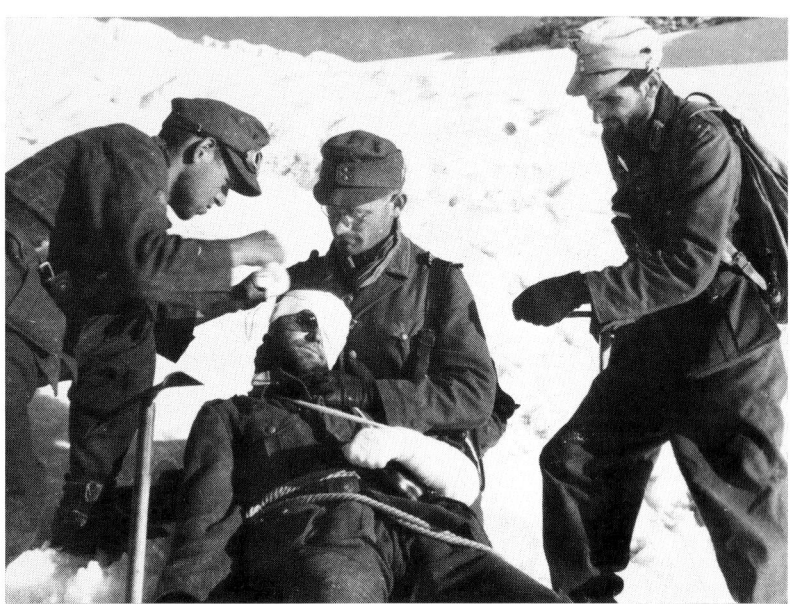

. . . and on bare rocks.

Isolated in the lonely mountains, the doctor and his aides work at a medical support point.

Stabsarzt Dr. Lins climbs over a wall of ice in the Dombai Ulgen.

The main bandaging station at Roshkovo in the Bolshaya-Laba Valley.

A bandaging station in the mud near Tuapse in the autumn of 1942.

Medical chests are packed before being parachuted.

The Paratroops

The first temporary bandage is put on an arm wound.

Who can, makes his way to the bandaging station, accompanied by slightly wounded comrades.

Carried on a stretcher by bearers, Sicily, 1943.

A gathering place for the wounded in the west, 1944.

Medical treatment at a troop bandaging station.

Stabsarzt Dr. Chors straightening an arm.

In Africa

On the way to the bandaging station.

On a tank that needs repairs—a captured wounded British soldier is carried too.

First aid in the desert.

A main bandaging station made only of tents.

At thirty degrees below zero—moved on an open sled, with only a blanket protecting from frostbite.

In the East and the West

First aid beside an armored scout car.

A nest of wounded in the winter of 1944-45.

Transport on an armored vehicle on the Italian front.

Horsedrawn wagons were the most frequent form of transport in Russia.

An overloaded Schützenpanzer carries slightly wounded men on the western front.

149

Wounded men make their way to a bandaging station on the eastern front.

Badly injured, exhausted and hopeless—a wounded man in the last weeks of the war.

The battalion doctor checks a bandaged Polish soldier in a ditch (Polish campaign, 1939).

Help for Wounded Enemies

A badly wounded French soldier has been taken from his shot-up tank and is carried to a bandaging station (western campaign, 1940).

Wounded British soldiers are carried by paratroops (Crete, 1941).

A German medical officer treats a wounded Russian soldier (Russian campaign, 1942).

Under the Red Cross flag: Germans and Americans rescue their wounded in 1944.

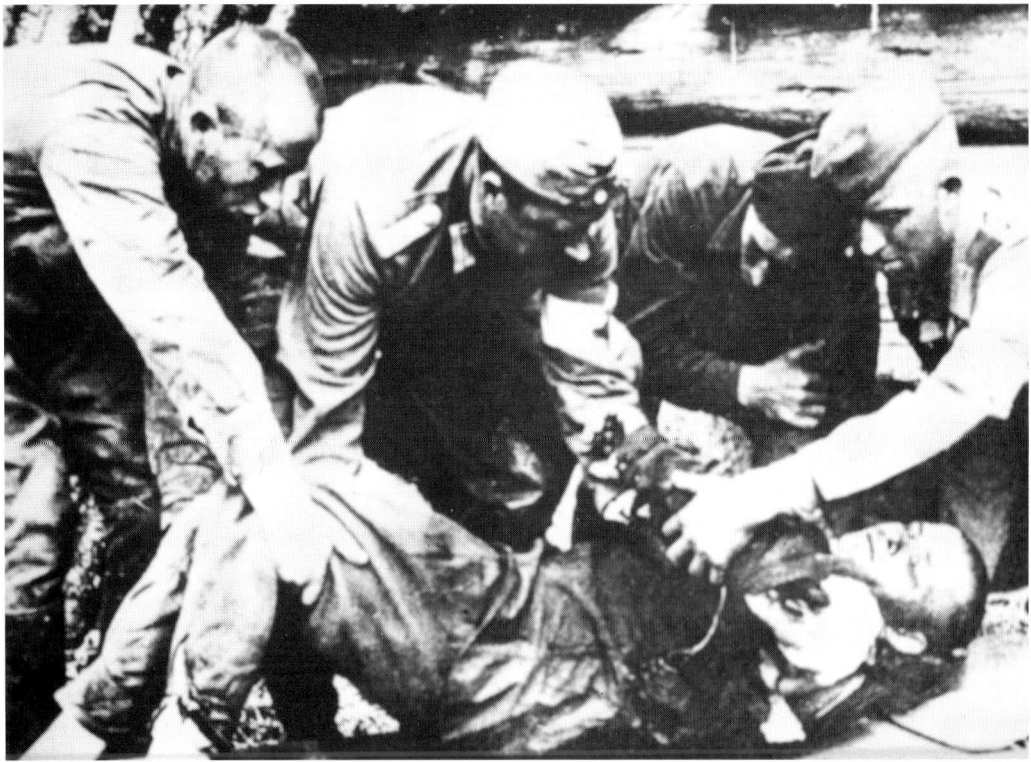